50トピックでトレーニング

英語で意見を言ってみる

Voice Your Opinions in English About 50 Topics

森 秀夫
Hideo Mori

はじめに

　日本では、少子高齢化社会による人口及び労働力の減少、**GDP** が世界で占める比率の縮小、外国人労働者の増加等が予想され、企業によっては、早くから、企業内英語公用語化を導入し、グローバル社会へ向けた対応をしています。グローバル社会では単に英会話ができるレベル、ニュースを聞いてわかる力だけでなく、英語で、論理的に思考し、議論する力が求められています。グローバル社会で生き残るためには、使える英語を身につけ、いろいろな国の人々と英語による意見の交換や議論をする必要があります。

　また、インターネット等、英語を学習する環境が整備され、日常の英会話ができる人は増えています。しかし、議論を少し深めようとすると、ネイティブスピーカーと同等に意見を言えません。時には、英語力不足から、ネイティブスピーカーの主張を受け入れるだけになってしまいます。

　日本人は、物事について英語で論理的に思考し、相手を説得することが苦手だとされ、これは、日本人の国民性や気質に起因するという人がいます。しかし、小学校から 10 年以上も英語を学び続けているにもかかわらず、日本人は、英語で自分の意見を相手に伝えて議論する場を、ほとんど与えられていません。結果として、建設的に自分の意見や主張を相手にしっかりと伝えることが苦手になっているだけなのです。

　本書では、そのような部分を補強するために、次のような工夫を凝らしています。

1. トピックは、**For or against? How? Which?** の3つのパターンです。例えば、「18歳選挙権の是非」「若さを維持する方法」「愛かお金か」等です。
2. 興味深いイラストで、ダイアローグの内容に関するイメージを膨らませます。
3. 賛否両論のトピックに関連した、50のダイアローグで興味や視野を拡大します。トピックについてよく考え、意見を持つことの重要性を再認識します。いろいろなトピックについて自分で考えることが英語の即興力につながります。
4. 重要な英単語・熟語は繰り返し解説してあり、1100の英単語・熟語集としても使えます。ダイアローグの内容を手がかりとして、トピックに関する単語や決まり文句が覚えやすくなります。

⑤ Tips には、よく使われる表現として I agree with you. 等、役に立つ表現に焦点を当てて、222の表現を学べます。
⑥ Tips で扱われる表現を含めて、意見を言う際に効果的な250の表現を学べます。なお、重要な表現は繰り返し解説してあります。
⑦ ダイアローグのトピックに関する250の英文を、自分の意見を言う際に活用できます。

　ジョンとダイアナが50のトピックについて賛成や反対の立場から意見を主張します。2人の意見は、正解が先にありきの意見ではなく、自分の主張する根拠に基づき、最適解を見いだすために意見を言っています。ある意味、人生は、常に選択や物事の是非について即興で意見を言ったり、提案したりすることの連続です。活用する際には、I understand his point, but... I don't think so because.... That's a bit extreme example.... のように、2人の意見を踏まえ、即興で自分が賛成や反対の意見を考え、提案する練習をしてください。また、自分の意見と比較しつつ、ダイアローグの内容を意見の一部として取り入れてください。2人の視点や価値観を踏まえて、自分の意見を考えることで、考える習慣・論理的思考力・批判力・判断力・分析力や問題解決力が身につきます。
　なお、50のダイアローグをとおして、意図的にハッキリと意見を言う設定にしてあります。しかし、英語では意見を言う際に、必ずしもハッキリ言うことが常に求められている訳ではありません。相手に対する配慮を表す言葉が必要になる場合があります。例えば、I disagree with you（あなたには賛成しない）の代わりに、I'm afraid I disagree with you. や I'm not sure if I support you. などと言います。また、「計画を変えるべきだ」という場合には、I think we should change the plan. などと言います。I'm afraid や I think など相手の意見を尊重する表現を意識すると良いでしょう。
　出版にあたり、企画段階から出版にいたるまでたくさんの方々に大変お世話になりました。そのおかげで、妥協することなく、新しいタイプのダイアローグ集を仕上げることができました。本当にありがとうございました。

2015年5月

著者　森　秀夫

CONTENTS

50トピックでトレーニング
英語で意見を言ってみる

はじめに 3

ケース❶ 喫煙者の権利の是非 12
　●よく使われる表現―反論①― 15

ケース❷ カジノの合法化の是非 17
　●よく使われる表現―反論②― 20

ケース❸ 美容整形手術の是非 22
　●よく使われる表現―反論③― 24

ケース❹ 義務投票制の是非 26
　●よく使われる表現―反論④― 29

ケース❺ 捕鯨の是非 31
　●よく使われる表現―反論⑤― 34

ケース❻ コンビニ24時間営業の是非 36
　●よく使われる表現―反論⑥― 39

ケース❼ 学校における金属探知機使用の是非 41
　●よく使われる表現―強調①― 44

ケース❽ 男性のメーキャップの是非 46
　●よく使われる表現―特に異存なし― 49

| ケース❾ | 校内スマホ禁止の是非　51 |
| | ●よく使われる表現―状況・場合―　54 |

| ケース❿ | 電車内優先席の是非　56 |
| | ●よく使われる表現―観点①―　59 |

| ケース⓫ | 暴力描写の多いテレビゲームの是非　61 |
| | ●よく使われる表現―強調②―　64 |

| ケース⓬ | 未成年者の門限の是非　66 |
| | ●よく使われる表現―強調③―　69 |

| ケース⓭ | 選挙権年齢の引き下げの是非　71 |
| | ●よく使われる表現―逆接①―　74 |

| ケース⓮ | 患者へのガン告知の是非　76 |
| | ●よく使われる表現―誤解―　79 |

| ケース⓯ | 小学1年生の通塾の是非　81 |
| | ●よく使われる表現―ためらい①―　83 |

| ケース⓰ | ダイエットの是非　85 |
| | ●よく使われる表現―ためらい②―　88 |

| ケース⓱ | サマータイムの是非　89 |
| | ●よく使われる表現―質問―　92 |

| ケース⓲ | 生徒のアルバイトの是非　94 |
| | ●よく使われる表現―確認①―　97 |

| ケース⓳ | ハイテクトイレの是非　99 |
| | ●よく使われる表現―確認②―　102 |

| ケース⑳ | 美人コンテストの是非　104 |
| | ●よく使われる表現―確認③―　106 |

| ケース㉑ | 救急車の有料化の是非　108 |
| | ●よく使われる表現―提案①―　111 |

| ケース㉒ | 小学校での英語教育の是非　113 |
| | ●よく使われる表現―理解―　116 |

| ケース㉓ | 動物実験の是非　118 |
| | ●よく使われる表現―一定の理解―　121 |

| ケース㉔ | 飲酒の是非　123 |
| | ●よく使われる表現―因果関係―　126 |

| ケース㉕ | 独身者のための結婚仲介業者の是非　128 |
| | ●よく使われる表現―理由①―　131 |

| ケース㉖ | 血液型と性格との関係の是非　133 |
| | ●よく使われる表現―感想・判断①―　136 |

| ケース㉗ | 女性に関する昇進の壁を破る方法　138 |
| | ●よく使われる表現―提案②―　141 |

| ケース㉘ | 笑いの力を効果的に利用する方法　143 |
| | ●よく使われる表現―言い換え①―　146 |

| ケース㉙ | 生徒のカンニングを防ぐ方法　148 |
| | ●よく使われる表現―賛成①―　151 |

| ケース㉚ | 若さを保つ方法　153 |
| | ●よく使われる表現―賛成②―　156 |

ケース㉛ 子供のテレビ視聴時間の制限方法　158
　　●よく使われる表現―結果―　161

ケース㉜ 個々のネチケットを確立する方法　163
　　●よく使われる表現―観点②―　166

ケース㉝ 地震の防災対策　168
　　●よく使われる表現―感想・判断②―　171

ケース㉞ 献血者の数を増やす方法　173
　　●よく使われる表現―賛成③―　176

ケース㉟ 良いスピーチの方法　178
　　●よく使われる表現―言い換え②―　180

ケース㊱ 家事を平等に分担する方法　182
　　●よく使われる表現―出典・参照―　185

ケース㊲ 飲料水の節約方法　187
　　●よく使われる表現―提案③―　190

ケース㊳ 英語力を身につける方法　192
　　●よく使われる表現―確認④―　195

ケース㊴ 食品廃棄物を減らす方法　197
　　●よく使われる表現―理由②―　199

ケース㊵ 退職する？　働き続ける？　201
　　●よく使われる表現―疑問―　204

ケース㊶ 新聞？　インターネット？　206
　　●よく使われる表現―理由③―　209

ケース㊷ 米？ パン？ 211
　●よく使われる表現―逆接②― 213

ケース㊸ 弁当？ 給食？ 215
　●よく使われる表現―追加― 218

ケース㊹ 愛？ お金？ 220
　●よく使われる表現―不明確さの指摘― 223

ケース㊺ 制服？ 私服？ 225
　●よく使われる表現―確認⑤― 228

ケース㊻ 都会生活？ 田舎生活？ 230
　●よく使われる表現―強調④― 233

ケース㊼ 猫派？ 犬派？ 235
　●よく使われる表現―反論⑦― 238

ケース㊽ 高価格のブランド製品？ 低価格のノーブランド製品？ 240
　●よく使われる表現―例― 243

ケース㊾ 独身？ 結婚？ 245
　●よく使われる表現―感想・判断③― 248

ケース㊿ カメ？ ウサギ？ 250
　●よく使われる表現―比較・対照― 253

●付属の MP3 CD-ROM について 255

50トピックでトレーニング
英語で意見を言ってみる

ケース 1
Track 1

喫煙者の権利の是非
Smokers' rights: for or against?

タバコの害は明白である。公共の場所で喫煙者のタバコを吸う権利を守ることは、必要なのだろうか。

ダイアローグ
Dialogue

TV anchor: One local government is planning to **ban** smoking in **public places such as** hotels, restaurants and the like. Owners of restaurants and hotels **fiercely object to** the plan. As a **compromise**, they may **be allowed to** have **enclosed** smoking sections.

ある地方自治体がホテルやレストランなどの公共の場所での喫煙を禁止する計画があります。レストランやホテルのオーナーはその計画に猛烈に反対しています。妥協案として、閉鎖された喫煙場所を設けることが許可されるかもしれません。

John: What do you think of this issue?

この問題についてどう思う？

ケース1　喫煙者の権利の是非

Diana: Well, **separating** smoking and nonsmoking sections seems to be a good idea. But, even so, some people will still have to work in an unhealthy environment. For example, workers in restaurants have to **serve customers** in smoking sections.

そうね。喫煙と禁煙場所を分けることは良いアイディアに思えるわ。しかしそれでも、不健康な環境で働かなくてはならない人がまだいるわ。例えばレストランで働く人たちは、喫煙場所で接客をしなくてはならないわ。

John: That's a bit **extreme**, isn't it? If you **insist on** such a point, no compromise can be made. If we **admit** what you say is a **valid argument**, we will have to ban smoking in public places **completely**. I can't support that.

それは、少し極端だね。もし、そんなことまで主張するなら、妥協点は見い出せないよ。もし君の言うことが議論するに値すると認めるなら、公共の場所での喫煙は完全に禁止しなくてはならないよ。それは支持できないな。

Diana: I don't think you get my point. Nobody has the right to **endanger** nonsmokers' health.

私の言いたいことがわかっていないわね。誰にも非喫煙者の健康を害する権利なんてないわ。

John: I disagree. Smokers' rights should be protected, too. I mean both smokers' rights and nonsmokers' rights should be protected equally, at least in public places.

僕は、賛成できないな。喫煙者の権利も守られるべきだね。つまり、喫煙者と非喫煙者、両者の権利は、少なくとも公共の場所では、平等に守られるべきだよ。

Diana: Listen, we used to **accept** smokers' rights, but their manners are terrible. For instance, I may be exaggerating, but smoking cigarettes while walking **results in** the **burning** of clothes and children's faces, and many smokers throw **cigarette butts** in the road. Besides, the majority of smokers don't even **care about** the **hazards** of second hand smoke to nonsmokers.

聞いてよ。私たちは、ずっと喫煙者の権利を受け入れてきたのよ。でも、彼らのマナーが最悪だったの。例えば、誇張かもしれないけど、歩きタバコで人の衣服を焦がしたり、子供の顔をやけどさせたりしているの。それに多くの人がタバコの吸い殻を道路に捨てたりしているの。それに、大多数の喫煙者は、非喫煙者の受動喫煙の危険性を気にさえしていないわ。

13

John: I see what you mean. In a sense, smokers **forfeit** their own rights by **violating** the rights of nonsmokers. To put it differently, you believe nonsmokers' rights are more important, right?

君の言いたいことはわかるよ。ある意味、喫煙者は、非喫煙者の権利を侵害することで、自分の権利を失っているんだ。違う言い方をすれば、君は非喫煙者の権利がより大切だと思っているんだね。

Diana: Absolutely right.

全くそのとおりよ。

Words & Phrases

- ban　〜を禁ずる
- public place　公共の場
- 〜 such as …　例えば…のような〜
- fiercely　激しく、猛烈に
- object to 〜　〜に反対する
- compromise　妥協、妥協する
- be allowed to 〜　〜することを許される
- enclosed　囲まれた
- separate　〜を分ける、別々の
- environment　環境
- serve　〜に尽くす、〜のために働く
- customer　顧客、お客
- extreme　極端な
- insist on 〜　〜を主張する
- and the like　〜など
- admit　〜を認める
- valid　妥当な、正当な
- argument　議論、論拠
- completely　完全に
- endanger　〜を危険にさらす
- accept　〜を受け入れる
- result in 〜　（結果的に）〜に終わる、〜をもたらす
- burn　〜をやけどする、〜を燃やす、〜を焦がす
- cigarette butt　タバコの吸い殻
- care about 〜　〜を気にかける
- hazard　危険
- forfeit　〜を剥奪される、〜を失う
- violate　〜を侵害する
- exaggerating　大げさに言う、誇張する
- in a sense　ある意味

ケース1　喫煙者の権利の是非

Tips　よく使われる表現―反論①―

- I disagree.
  （反対である。）
- I can't support your idea.
  （あなたの意見を支持できない。）
- I can't back you up on this matter.
  （この件について、あなたの意見を支持できない。）
- I'm not going to support you on this issue.
  （この件について、あなたを支持しない。）
- I'm not in favor of it.
  （私はそれに賛成しない。）

◆その他の表現

- What do you think of this issue?
  （この問題をどう思うの？）
- I can't support that.
  （私にはそれを受け入れられない。）
- I don't think you get my point.
  （私の意図がわかっていないと思う。）
- I may be exaggerating a little bit, but ～
  （ちょっと大げさかもしれないが～）
- I see what you mean.
  （あなたの言いたいことはわかる。）
- to put it differently
  （違う言い方をすれば）

◆すぐに使える表現　Possible Opinions

- [ ] It's time to raise the price of cigarettes.
  （タバコの値段を上げる時期である。）
- [ ] Let people know tobacco damages their health and others' by showing pictures and statements on cigarette packs.
  （タバコのパッケージに写真やメッセージを載せて、タバコが自分と他人の健康を害することを知らせよう。）
- [ ] It's time for the government to take strong action and declare a ban on smoking in public places.
  （政府は、思い切った対策を打ち出し、公共の場所における喫煙の禁止を宣言すべき時期である。）
- [ ] It's time to impose fines on people who smoke in public places.
  （公共の場所で喫煙した人に罰金を科すべき時期である。）
- [ ] It's scientifically proven that smoking is bad for our health.
  （喫煙が健康に悪いことは科学的に証明されている。）
- [ ] People have the right to choose their own lifestyle.
  （人々は自分の生き方を選ぶ権利がある。）
- [ ] Tobacco suppresses one's appetite, so it's good for those who are overweight.
  （タバコは人の食欲を抑制してくれる。だから、太りすぎの人には良い。）

ケース 2　カジノの合法化の是非
Track 2
Legalizing casinos: for or against?

地域の活性化を図るためにカジノの合法化が検討されている。ギャンブル依存症などの問題のあるカジノは必要なのだろうか。

ダイアローグ
Dialogue

TV anchor: This year, a **blitz** of new Las Vegas–style casinos made Macao the world's top gambling **hub** in **revenue**. In Macao, there are so many rich people that money **no longer seems like** money there.

今年は、新しいラスベガススタイルのカジノの攻勢のおかげで、マカオは収益で世界一のギャンブルの中心になりました。マカオでは、あまりにも多く金持ちがいて、そこでは、お金がお金でないようにみえます。

Diana: Did you know the revenue of casinos in Macao **exceeded** that of Las Vegas this year?

今年マカオのカジノの収益がラスベガスの収益を超えたって知っていた?

John: No. I **was unaware of** that. Businesses in

いや。それには気づかな

Las Vegas seem to be much bigger than those in Macao. Besides, Las Vegas not only has casinos, but also other forms of **entertainment** such as **exhibitions**, shopping malls, hotels and **big-name** shows. I'm surprised to find out that Macao **takes in** more money.

かったね。マカオよりラスベガスのビジネスの方がよっぽど大きいように思うけど。しかも、ラスベガスにはカジノだけでなく、見本市、シッピングモール、ホテル、有名なショーなどの娯楽の形態があるからね。マカオがより多くのお金を集めているなんて驚きだね。

Diana: Me, too. Speaking of casinos, are you for **legalizing** casinos in Japan?

私もよ。カジノと言えば、日本におけるカジノの合法化についてあなたは賛成なの？

John: Yes, I am, as a matter of fact. I think people nowadays **get stressed out** from work. Gambling can be a good way to relax. Once **refreshed**, they will be more motivated to work. **In this respect**, I agree that casinos should be legalized.

実は、賛成さ。最近人々は仕事でストレスを抱えすぎていると思うし。ギャンブルはリラックスする一つの良い方法になるしね。いったんリフレッシュすれば、働く意欲も湧くよ。この点で、カジノが合法化されることに賛成さ。

Diana: Actually, I don't agree with you. Japan already has legalized gambling in horse and bicycle racing. Why do we have to have more gambling? A lot of people, especially the poor, tend to gamble more money than they earn. They **get addicted to** gambling and stop working. Most of them have families, and **sooner or later**, they may **suffer from** a **family breakdown** or become **social dropouts**.

実を言うと、私はあなたに賛成ではないわ。日本にはすでに合法化された競馬や競輪のギャンブルがあるのよ。どうして、さらにギャンブルが必要なの。多くの人々、特に貧しい人々は、稼ぐ以上に多くのお金を賭ける傾向にあるわ。彼らはギャンブル中毒になって働くことをやめてしまうの。ほとんどの人々には家族があって遅かれ早かれ、家庭崩壊に陥るか、社会の落伍者になってしまうわ。

John: Don't only look at the bad sides of gambling! Casinos create new businesses and more jobs.

ギャンブルの悪い側面だけ見ることはやめなよ。カジノはより多くの新し

ケース2　カジノの合法化の是非

Even if people lose some money, they have other chances to **earn** more money.

いビジネスや仕事を生み出すのさ。人々がお金を失っても、より多くのお金を稼ぐチャンスがあるんだ。

Diana: You're missing the big picture. I have seen casinos cause some people to **gamble away** not only their money but also their lives.

あなたは、全体像を見失っているわ。私はカジノが原因で何人もの人がお金だけでなく命を失なうのを見てきたわ。

Words & Phrases

- blitz　猛攻撃
- hub　中心
- revenue　収益、財源
- no longer ～　もはや～ない
- seem like ～　～のようである
- exceed　～を超える
- be unaware of ～　～に気がつかない
- entertainment　娯楽
- exhibition　見本市、展覧会
- big-name　有名な、一流の
- take in ～　（金など）～を集める
- legalize　～を公認する、～を法律上正当と認める
- get stressed out ～　～でストレスがたまる
- (get) refreshed　元気を回復する、さわやかな気分になる
- in this respect　この点に関して
- get addicted to ～　～中毒になる
- sooner or later　遅かれ早かれ
- suffer from ～　～で苦しむ
- family breakdown　家庭崩壊
- social dropout　社会からの落伍者
- earn　～を稼ぐ
- gamble away ～　～を賭事で失う

> **Tips** よく使われる表現―反論②―

☐ You're missing the big picture.
　（あなたは、全体像を見失っている。）
☐ Your opinion lacks something.
　（あなたの意見は何か欠けている。）
☐ You're ignoring something important.
　（あなたは何か重要なことを見落としている。）
☐ You're not looking at the bigger issue.
　（あなたはより大きな問題を見ていない。）

◆ その他の表現

☐ speaking of ～
　（～と言えば）
☐ Are you for legalizing casinos in Japan?
　（日本におけるカジノの合法化については賛成なの。）
☐ as a matter of fact
　（実は）
☐ In this respect, I agree that casinos should be legalized.
　（この点でカジノが合法化されることに賛成である。）
☐ I don't agree with you.
　（私はあなたに賛成しない。）

◆すぐに使える表現　Possible Opinions

- [ ] It's likely that people could lose themselves completely in casino gambling.
  （人々はカジノのギャンブルで完全に自分を見失うことがありそうだ。）
- [ ] Casinos give people dreams of getting rich quick.
  （カジノは人々に一攫千金の夢を与える。）
- [ ] Is there a link between casino gambling and a rise in the crime rate?
  （カジノのギャンブルと犯罪発生率の増加に関連はあるの？）
- [ ] Casino gambling may attract a lot of tourists.
  （カジノのギャンブルが多くの旅行者を引きつけるかもしれない。）
- [ ] Cities could collect a large amount of tax revenue.
  （市は多額の税収を確保できるであろう。）
- [ ] Casino gambling could cause an increase in crime and criminal activities.
  （カジノのギャンブルは、罪や犯罪活動の増加を引き起こしうる。）
- [ ] Casinos should not be legal because it could break apart families.
  （カジノは家族を崩壊させうるので、合法化すべきでない。）

ケース 3 美容整形手術の是非
Track 3 Cosmetic surgery: for or against?

最近は、美容整形手術に対する抵抗感は低くなっている。一度変えたら二度と元に戻れない美容整形手術は必要なのだろうか。

ダイアローグ
Dialogue

TV anchor: South Korea's **reputation regarding** cosmetic surgery is well known. According to a survey, 60 percent of **respondents** aged 18 to 24 have had cosmetic surgery. In fact, it's very **common** for **graduating students** to have surgery before **job hunting**.

> 美容整形手術に関する韓国の評判はよく知られています。ある調査によれば、18歳から24歳までの回答者の60パーセントが美容整形手術を受けたことがあります。実際、卒業予定者が就活前に手術を受けることが普通に行われています。

John: Do you agree with the **practice** of cosmetic surgery?

> あなたは美容整形手術を行うことに賛成なの？

ケース3　美容整形手術の是非

Diana: Don't ask me such a question! I'm **satisfied with** the way I look. This is me. I am **comfortable with** who I am. What about you?

私にそんな質問をしないでよ。私は自分の見た目には満足しているの。これが私なの。今の自分に満足しているの。あなたはどうなの？

John: Me? I don't need a **perfect** face. I am, however, not 100% satisfied with the way I look.

僕？僕は完璧な顔を必要とはしないよ。でも、自分の見た目に100パーセント満足はしていないよ。

Diana: Do you want to have some changes made to your face?

自分の顔で変えたいところはあるの？

John: **To some extent**, yes. For instance, I want to **remove my crow's feet**, and I want to **enlarge** the size of my eyes. Then I don't think I would **be so concerned about** my appearance. Such surgery not only makes one look better, but also **boosts one's confidence**. I think making small changes is **acceptable**, like enlarging the size of one's eyes.

ある程度、そうだね。例えば、目尻のシワは取り除きたいね。それで、目の大きさも大きくしたいな。そうすれば、自分の外見については気にならなくなると思うね。手術は、見た目を良くするだけでなく、自信を高めてくれるしね。目の大きさを大きくするような少しの変更なら許容範囲だと思うよ。

Diana: I don't agree with you. We have **traits** we **inherited from** our **ancestors**. Our bodies are part of our **identity**. We should love the way we are.

私はそうは思わないわ。私たちは祖先から受け継いだ特徴があるのよ。私たちの体は私たちのアイデンティティの一部よ。今のありのままの姿を愛すべきよ。

John: Don't you understand why students in Korea decide to have cosmetic surgery before job hunting? Companies tend to hire the **better-looking applicant** if two applicants have

韓国の学生が、なぜ就活前に美容整形手術を受ける決断をするかわからないのかい。企業は仮に2人の応募者がほぼ同じ能力を持っていれば、見た目の良い応募者を雇う傾

23

nearly **identical** abilities. They don't want to lose **opportunities** due to their **unattractive** traits.

向にあるからさ。学生達は魅力のない特徴のせいでチャンスを失いたくないのさ。

Diana: Just remember, after such surgery, your face is changed forever.

手術後は、あなたの顔が永遠に変わってしまうことを忘れないでね。

Words & Phrases

- ☐ reputation　評判
- ☐ regarding　～に関して、～について
- ☐ respondent　回答者
- ☐ common　ふつうの、一般的な
- ☐ graduating student　卒業予定者
- ☐ job hunt　求職する、仕事を探す
- ☐ practice　実行、実施
- ☐ be satisfied with ～　～に満足である
- ☐ be comfortable with ～　～に満足である、快適である
- ☐ perfect　完璧な、完全な
- ☐ to some extent　ある程度まで
- ☐ remove one's crow's feet　目尻のシワを取り除く
- ☐ enlarge　～を大きくする
- ☐ be concerned about ～　～を気にかける、～を心配する
- ☐ boost one's confidence　～の自信を高める
- ☐ acceptable　受け入れられる、容認可能な
- ☐ trait　特徴、特質
- ☐ inherit from ～　～から受け継ぐ
- ☐ ancestor　祖先
- ☐ identity　本人であること、自己同一性
- ☐ better-looking　より良い顔つきの
- ☐ applicant　志願者、応募者
- ☐ identical　（あらゆる点で）同一の、全く同じ
- ☐ opportunity　機会、チャンス
- ☐ unattractive　見た目がさえない、魅力のない

Tips　よく使われる表現—反論③—

☐ **I don't agree with you.**
　（あなたの意見には賛成しない。）

☐ I'm not in favor of your opinion.
（私はあなたの意見に賛成しない。）
☐ I don't approve of what you're suggesting.
（私はあなたの提案していることを認めない。）
☐ I don't agree to that.
（私はそれに賛成しない。）

◆その他の表現

☐ according to a survey
（ある調査によると）
☐ Do you agree with the practice of cosmetic surgery?
（あなたは美容整形手術を行うことに賛成なの？）
☐ for instance
（例えば）

◆すぐに使える表現　Possible Opinions

☐ Cosmetic surgery is not free from problems and unwanted aftereffects.
（美容整形手術では、いろいろな問題や望んでいない後遺症の可能性が全くないわけではない。）
☐ Nobody can stop aging.
（誰も老いを止めることはできない。）
☐ The quest for youth and beauty will never disappear.
（若さと美の追究は決してなくならない。）
☐ Regardless of surgery, people can't stop aging.
（手術をしたとしても、人々は老いを止めることはできない。）
☐ Some patients won't be satisfied with their looks after plastic surgery due to high expectations.
（美容整形手術による期待感が高いため、自分の顔に満足しない患者がいる。）

ケース 4 義務投票制の是非

Track 4　A compulsory voting system: for or against?

義務投票制を導入して90％以上の投票率を維持している国がある。民主政治には義務投票制は必要なのだろうか。

ダイアローグ
Dialogue

TV anchor: The Japanese **Diet election took place** last Sunday. According to the **election board**, the final **voting rate** was about 53%. It was one of the lowest **voter turnouts** of the past two **decades**. The election board is discussing what Japan should do to **raise voters' interest** in elections.

日本の国会議員選挙が先週の日曜日に開催されました。選挙管理委員会によれば、最終投票率はおよそ53％で、過去20年間で最低レベルでした。選挙管理委員会は日本が有権者の選挙への関心を高めるために、何をすべきか議論しています。

Diana: Why don't people vote in elections?

なぜ人々は選挙で投票しないのかしら？

ケース4　義務投票制の是非

John: Many of them are not very interested in **politics**, I suppose. To make matters worse, they think politics is **none of their business**.

彼らの多くは、政治に興味がないからだと思うよ。さらに悪いことに、政治が自分たちと関係がないと思っているんだ。

Diana: Really? I'm surprised. The right to vote is given to anyone 20 years old and over, isn't it? It's **strange** for them to **abstain from** this right.

本当なの？私は驚いたわ。選挙する権利は20歳以上の全ての人に与えられるのよね。この権利を放棄するなんて不思議ね。

John: People have the right to vote, but it's not **compulsory** in Japan.

人々に選挙権はあるけど、日本では義務ではないんだ。

Diana: **In order to** raise voting rates, isn't it a good idea to **fine** people who don't vote in elections?

投票率を伸ばすために、選挙で投票しない人に罰金を科すのは良い考えだと思わない？

John: I don't think so. **To reiterate**, it's not compulsory. Moreover, voting rates are **not always** this low. Raising voting rates **is** not necessarily **directly related to** raising voters' interest in politics.

僕はそう思わないよ。繰り返し言うけど、それは、義務でないんだ。投票率がいつもこれほど低い訳じゃないから。投票率を伸ばすことが、投票者の政治への関心を高めることと必ずしも直接結びついてないしね。

Diana: I think you are wrong on that point. Even if people are being made to vote in elections, they might become more interested in politics. If they feel their **opinions** have been heard, for instance, they might become more interested. Besides, voting in elections doesn't only mean choosing members of the Diet, but also means **sharing** their opinions

私はその点ではあなたが間違っていると思うわ。たとえ、人々が選挙で投票させられたとしても、より政治に関心を持つかもしれないわ。例えば、人々が自分の意見が届いたと感じたら、もっと関心を示すかもしれないわ。それに、選挙で投票することは、国会議員を選ぶことを意味するだけではなく、自分たちの意見を他の人と共有することを意味するの。

with others.

John: I understand your point. However, I still feel uncomfortable fining people who don't vote. 君の言いたいことはわかるよ。でも、投票しない人々に罰金を科すことに僕は違和感を覚えるよ。

Words & Phrases

- Diet election　国会議員選挙
- take place　開催される
- election board　選挙管理委員会
- voting rate　投票率
- voter turnout　投票率、全投票者数
- decade　10年間
- raise voters' interest　投票者の関心を高める
- politics　政治
- none of one's business　〜にかかわりのないこと
- strange　（変で）驚くべき、奇妙な
- abstain from 〜　〜を棄権する、〜を慎む
- compulsory　強制的な、義務的な
- in order to 〜　〜するために
- fine　〜に罰金を科する
- to reiterate　繰り返し言うが
- not always　いつも〜であるとは限らない
- directly　直接に
- be related to 〜　〜に関係がある
- opinion　意見
- share… with 〜　〜と…を分かち合う、〜と…を共有する

ケース４　義務投票制の是非

Tips　よく使われる表現―反論④―

☐ You are wrong on that point.
　（あなたはその点では間違っている。）
☐ What you said is wrong.
　（あなたが言っていたことは間違いだ。）
☐ That's not true.
　（それは、真実ではない。）
☐ You're terribly mistaken.
　（あなたはひどい勘違いをしている。）
☐ You've got it all wrong.
　（あなたはまるっきり勘違いしている。）

◆その他の表現

☐ to make matters worse
　（さらに悪いことには）
☐ I don't think so.
　（そう思わない。）
☐ moreover
　（さらに）
☐ besides
　（その上、さらに）
☐ I understand your point.
　（あなたの考えを理解する。）

◆すぐに使える表現　Possible Opinions

- ☐ It's important to raise the voting rate in order to improve the quality of the government.
（政治の質を改善するために、投票率を上げることが重要である。）
- ☐ If we don't vote in elections, the right to vote becomes meaningless.
（選挙で投票しないと、投票権を持っている意味がなくなる。）
- ☐ A system of fining non-voters should be adopted in order to raise voters' interest in elections and politics.
（投票しない人に罰金を科すシステムは、有権者の選挙と政治への関心を高めるために取り入れるべきである。）
- ☐ Fining non-voters will not increase interest in politics.
（投票しない人に罰金を科しても、政治への関心は高まらない。）
- ☐ Mandatory voting is not a real solution. First, we should figure out the reason why people don't vote and address the cause of this problem.
（義務投票制は、本当の解決策ではない。最初に、なぜ人々が投票しないのかその理由を解明し、この問題の原因に取り組むべきである。）
- ☐ In Australia, mandatory voting became law in 1924.
（オーストラリアでは、義務投票制が1924年に立法化された。）

ケース 5 捕鯨の是非
Track 5　Whale hunting: for or against?

基本的に種の絶滅につながる生物の捕獲は許されない。鯨は絶滅危惧種に該当し保護すべきなのだろうか。

ダイアローグ
Dialogue

TV anchor: An **environmental protection group** has been **obstructing** whale hunting **fleets** again by **throwing** bottles of **acid** onto the decks of ships. The group **insists**, **as long as** they are **chasing** the fleets, hunters are not killing whales.

環境保護団体が、酸の入った瓶を船のデッキに投げて捕鯨船を妨害しています。団体が捕鯨船を追っている限り、捕鯨船に鯨は殺せないと団体は主張しています。

John: What do you think of this issue?

この問題をどう思う?

Diana: I totally disagree with whale hunting. In spite

私は捕鯨に全く同意しな

of that, I admit the environmental protection group's actions are not right.

いわ。それでも、環境保護団体の行動が正しくないと思うわ。

John: I don't support the environmental protection group because their arguments are not **consistent**. First they insist whales **are in danger of extinction**. Then, when they find the number of whales increasing, they say whales are very clever. The next day, they say killing whales is **cruel**.

僕は環境保護団体を支持しない、というのも、彼らの議論に一貫性がないからなんだ。最初、鯨は絶滅の危機に瀕していると主張した。次に、鯨の数が増えているとわかった時、鯨はとても賢いと主張し、次の日には、鯨を殺すことは残酷だと主張しているんだ。

Diana: You're right. But I don't see the average Japanese eating whale meat **on a daily basis**. I think there is no actual need for Japanese to eat whale meat anymore. Why don't we leave the whales alone?

そうね。でも、ふつうの日本人が日常的に鯨肉を食べているのを見かけないの。日本人が鯨肉を食べる実際の必要性はないと思うの。どうして鯨をそっとしてあげないのかしら？

John: That would surely cause serious problems. Statistically speaking, whales are the world's biggest **mammals** and they eat various sea **creatures** at more than 3 times the **volume** that humans do.

そうすると間違いなく深刻な問題を生じるからさ。統計的に言うと、鯨は最も大きな哺乳動物で、人間が食べる3倍以上も海の様々な生き物を食べるんだ。

Diana: Really? I have never heard such statistics. What might happen if the number of whales **continues to** rise?

本当？そんな統計は聞いたことないわ。もし鯨の数が増え続けるとどうなるのかしら。

John: The whales will surely destroy the **ecosystems** of the oceans by eating a lot of **sardines**,

たくさんのイワシ、エビなどを食うことで、鯨は確実に海の生態系を壊すね。

shrimps, and so forth.

Diana: So you support whale hunting. You know, I find myself agreeing with you now.

> じゃ、あなたは、捕鯨には賛成なのね。私も今じゃあなたに賛成よ。

Words & Phrases

- environmental protection group　環境保護団体
- obstruct　～を妨害する
- fleet　船団、艦隊
- throw　～を投げる
- acid　酸
- insist　～を主張する
- as long as ～　～する限り（間）は
- chase　～を追跡する
- consistent　一貫した
- be in danger of ～　～の危険がある、～しそうである
- extinction　絶滅
- cruel　残酷な、むごい、痛ましい
- on a daily basis　日常的に
- mammal　哺乳動物
- creature　生き物
- volume　量
- continue to ～　～することを続ける
- ecosystem　生態系
- sardine　イワシ
- shrimp　小エビ、エビ
- and so forth　～など

Tips よく使われる表現 ―反論⑤―

- ☐ I totally disagree with whale hunting.
  (私は捕鯨に絶対反対である。)
- ☐ I disagree with your idea.
  (あなたの考えに反対する。)
- ☐ I'm opposed to your opinion.
  (あなたの意見に反対である。)
- ☐ I have a different opinion.
  (私は違う意見を持っている。)
- ☐ That's not the way I see it.
  (それは私の見解と違う。)

◆その他の表現

- ☐ What do you think of this issue?
  (この問題についてどう思う？)
- ☐ in spite of that
  (それにもかかわらず)
- ☐ I don't support the environmental protection group because their arguments are not consistent.
  (彼らの議論に一貫性がないので、環境保護団体を支持しない。)
- ☐ cause
  (〜の原因となる、〜を（結果として）引き起こす)
- ☐ statistically speaking
  (統計的に言うと)
- ☐ So you support whale hunting.
  (それで捕鯨を支持するのかい。)

ケース 5　捕鯨の是非

> ◆すぐに使える表現　Possible Opinions

- ☐ Eating whale meat is a traditional aspect of Japanese culture.
  （鯨肉を食べることは、日本文化の伝統的側面である。）
- ☐ Whale meat is a good source of protein.
  （鯨肉は良いタンパク源である。）
- ☐ Why don't people feel pity for cattle, pigs and chickens?
  （なぜ人々は牛、豚、鶏に対しては同情しないの？）
- ☐ Other animals can be raised by human beings and their numbers increased, but whales cannot.
  （他の動物は人間によって養殖可能で、数を増やせる。しかし、鯨は増やせない。）
- ☐ People eat cows, sheep, kangaroos, alligators, dogs and so on according to their culture.
  （人々は、文化によっては、牛、羊、カンガルー、ワニ、犬などを食べる。）
- ☐ Whales don't reproduce quickly. Further hunting may wipe out the species.
  （鯨はすぐには繁殖しない。さらなる捕鯨は種を絶滅させるかもしれない。）

ケース6 コンビニ24時間営業の是非

Track 6

24-hour convenience stores: for or against?

⁉ 環境問題対策や治安改善のためコンビニの深夜営業を規制する動きがある。コンビニの深夜営業は、本当に必要なのだろうか。

ダイアローグ
Dialogue

TV anchor: The Kyoto **Protocol requires** industrialized countries to cut **greenhouse gas emissions**. Under this **agreement**, in order to reduce **carbon dioxide emissions**, some **local governments** are planning to ask **convenience stores** to **refrain from** staying open 24 hours a day.

京都議定書では、先進国に温室効果ガスの排出を削減することが求められています。この協定のもとで二酸化炭素の排出を削減するために、コンビニに24時間営業を控えるように依頼する計画をしている地方自治体があります。

John: What do you think about this issue?

この問題についてどう思う？

ケース6　コンビニ24時間営業の是非

Diana: I think it's a bad idea. Convenience stores offer safe shelter for women when they feel threatened especially at night.

私は悪い考えだと思うわ。コンビニは女性が、特に夜に危険だと感じた時に安全なシェルターとなってくれるの。

John: What you just said is true, but, on the other hand, convenience stores sometimes become targets for **robberies** at night. A convenience store used for shelter could actually become **quite** dangerous. Also, **unsavory** people tend to **gather** at convenience stores at night. Sometimes even I **feel scared**.

君が今言ったことは事実だけど、一方では、コンビニは時々、夜に泥棒の標的になるよ。シェルターとして使われるコンビニが実際にはかなり危険になり得るね。また、不良が夜になるとそこに集まる傾向にあるよ。僕でさえ時々怖い思いをするよ。

Diana: Still, I feel relieved to find convenience stores open at night. Furthermore, 24-hour convenience stores play an important role in the lives of **those who** work at night and sleep during the daytime. For example, such people are able to pay their **bills and taxes** there.

それでも、私は夜にコンビニがあいているとホッとするわ。さらに夜働いて日中寝ている人の生活にとって、24時間営業のコンビニが果たす役割は重要だわ。例えば、コンビニでは請求書や税金を払うことができるの。

John: What you're saying is a little extreme. Such people can **take a day off** to accomplish such **errands**. In addition, these days, it's common to use **automatic transfer services** at the bank to pay such bills.

君が言っていることは少し極端だよ。そのような人々だって用事を済ませるために、休暇を取ることができる。さらに、最近は、そんな請求書の支払いをするのに、銀行の自動振替サービスを利用するのが一般的だよね。

Diana: Even if convenience stores **shorten** their **business hours**, they still have to operate large **refrigerators** at night. **It makes no**

たとえコンビニの営業時間を短くしたとしても、夜に大きな冷蔵庫を稼働させなきゃいけないわ。ガスの排出に関しては変わらないわ。

difference in terms of gas emissions.

John: If that's what you think, you're terribly mistaken. Taking small steps **in the right direction** is **crucial**.

もしそれが君の考えることなら、君はひどい勘違いをしている。正しい方向に小さなステップを積み重ねることが重要なんだよ。

Diana: You may be right. But remember, many people will **lose their jobs** if convenience stores reduce business hours, and local governments don't want to put people **out of work** in this **recession**.

あなたは正しいかもしれない。でも、覚えておいてね。もしコンビニが営業時間を縮めれば、多くの人々が仕事を失うわ。そして、地方自治体は、この不景気に人々が失業になることを望まないわ。

Words & Phrases

- protocol　議定書
- require　〜を要求する
- greenhouse gas emission　温室効果ガス排出
- agreement　協定
- carbon dioxide emission　二酸化炭素排出
- local government　地方自治体
- convenience store　コンビニ
- refrain from 〜　〜を控える、〜を慎む
- robbery　強盗
- quite　かなり
- unsavory　いかがわしい、怪しい
- gather　集まる
- feel scared　おびえる、恐怖感を持つ
- those who 〜　〜する人々
- bills and taxes　請求書や税金
- take a day off　1日休暇を取る
- errand　用事
- automatic transfer service　自動振替サービス
- shorten business hours　営業時間を短くする
- refrigerator　冷蔵庫
- It makes no difference.　違いが生じない、重要ではない
- in terms of 〜　〜の観点から、〜によって
- in the right direction　正しい方向に
- crucial　決定的な、きわめて重大な
- lose one's job　仕事を失う
- (be) out of work　失業中で（ある）
- recession　不景気

> **Tips** よく使われる表現 ― 反論⑥ ―

- What you're saying is a little extreme.
  （あなたの言っていることは少し極端である。）
- Don't you think you may be exaggerating a bit?
  （あなたは少し誇張していると思わないかい？）
- I think your statement is extreme.
  （あなたの言っていることは極端だと思う。）
- Aren't you being a little harsh?
  （ちょっと言い過ぎじゃない？）

◆その他の表現

- What do you think about this issue?
  （この問題についてどう思う。）
- I think it's a bad idea.
  （それは悪い考えだと思う。）
- What you just said is true, but ～ .
  （あなたが今言ったことは正しいが、～。）
- in addition
  （加えて、さらに）
- If that's what you think, you're terribly mistaken.
  （もしそれがあなたの考えることなら、ひどい勘違いである。）
- You may be right.
  （あなたが正しいかもしれない。）

◆すぐに使える表現　Possible Opinions

- ☐ Convenience stores waste large amounts of fresh food through expiration dates alone.
  （コンビニは、賞味期限が過ぎたという理由だけで多くの生鮮食品を廃棄する。）
- ☐ Areas around convenience stores can become noisy because lots of people gather there at night.
  （コンビニの周りは、夜にたくさんの人々が集まり騒がしくなる。）
- ☐ Most people get up in the morning and come home from work and sleep at night. Generally, they don't go to convenience stores at midnight.
  （多くの人は朝起きて、夜仕事から帰って眠る。普通は、真夜中にコンビニに行ったりしない。）
- ☐ It's convenient that we can buy food or drinks whenever we want.
  （買いたい時にいつでも、食べ物や飲み物を買えれば便利である。）
- ☐ We can buy concert tickets or pay bills anytime at a convenience store.
  （コンビニでいつでもコンサートのチケットを買ったり請求書の支払いをしたりすることができる。）

ケース 7　学校における金属探知機使用の是非

Track 7　Using metal detectors in schools: for or against?

アメリカでは学校における発砲乱射事件が起きており、対抗措置として金属探知機を導入している。学校における金属探知機は必要なのだろうか。

ダイアローグ
Dialogue

TV anchor: About **two decades ago**, the **shooting** at Columbine high school surprised the world. Since then, hundreds of schools have **installed tighter security systems** such as **surveillance cameras** and **metal detectors**. Some schools have also **hired security guards**. With these **measures taken**, the number of crimes in schools has been greatly **reduced**.

約20年前、コロンバイン高校での銃撃事件が世界を震撼させました。その時以来、何百という学校で、監視カメラや金属探知機などの厳重なセキュリティシステムが導入されています。警備員を雇用している学校もあります。これらの手段を講じて、校内犯罪件数は、劇的に減少しています。

John:	That's a big **burden** on schools. It must cost **a huge amount of money** to install metal detectors.	それは、学校にとって大きな負担だね。金属探知機を設置するには多額の費用がかかるに違いない。
Diana:	Yeah, it's very expensive. These are measures mainly taken for a few students whose **behavior** is **out of control**. Do you agree with these measures?	ええ、かなりの額よ。これらの手段は主に、手がつけられない行為の生徒に対してとられたのよ。これらの手段には賛成なの？
John:	Yes, I do. They are **worth** the security they provide. The number of crimes in school has greatly **decreased**. Metal detectors have **played a large role in discouraging** students from bringing **weapons** into school. We should introduce metal detectors into every school.	賛成さ。セキュリティシステムを設置する価値はあるよ。校内犯罪件数は劇的に減少したよ。金属探知機は生徒が武器を学校へ持ち込むことを阻止するのに大きな役割を果たしているよ。金属探知機は全学校に導入すべきだね。
Diana:	Do you really think metal detectors can stop students from bringing in weapons?	本当に金属探知機が生徒の武器持ち込みを阻止できると思っているの？
John:	Yeah, why not?	そうだよ、何で？
Diana:	I admit they have some effect, but those students will try to bring in weapons regardless of metal detectors. The result will be the same **no matter what** security measures are taken.	いくらかの効果は上げていると認めるけど、それらの生徒は、金属探知機の有無にかかわらず、持ち込もうとするでしょう。どれだけセキュリティシステムが講じられようと、結果は同じよ。
John:	I still think metal detectors help to **prevent** fear of crimes among students. They can	僕は、金属探知機は犯罪を恐れる生徒の恐怖心を取り除くのに役立っていると思う。心配しないで

ケース7　学校における金属探知機使用の是非

concentrate on their studies **without worrying**. What do you think?

勉強に集中できるよ。どう思う？

Diana: Well, in addition to the use of metal detectors, I think what counts most is for teachers to listen to students more and try to understand **what makes** them **tick**.

そうね。金属探知機の活用に加えて、最も大切なことは、教師が生徒にもっと耳を傾け、何が彼らを犯罪に駆り立てるのかを理解しようとすることよ。

Words & Phrases

- two decades ago　20年前
- shooting　発砲
- install tight security systems　厳重なセキュリティシステムを取り付ける
- surveillance camera　監視カメラ
- metal detector　金属探知機
- hire security guards　警備員を雇う
- take a measure to ～　～する措置をとる
- reduce　減る
- burden　負担、重荷
- a huge amount of money　多額のお金
- behavior　行動
- out of control　手に負えない
- worth　～する価値がある
- decrease　減る
- play a large role in ～　～において大きな役割を果たす
- discourage　～をやめさせる、～を思いとどまらせる
- weapon　武器
- no matter what ～　たとえどんな～であろうとも
- prevent　～を抑える、～を妨げる
- concentrate on ～　～に集中する
- without worrying　心配せずに
- what makes ～ tick　～を行動させる動機

43

Tips よく使われる表現―強調①―

- [ ] what counts most is ～
  （最も大切なことは～である）
- [ ] it is important to note that ～
  （～に注目することは大切である）
- [ ] most importantly (of all) ～
  （最も大切なことは～）
- [ ] what matters is that ～
  （大切なことは～である）
- [ ] the name of the game is that ～
  （肝心なことは～である）

◆ その他の表現

- [ ] Do you agree with these measures?
  （これらの措置に賛成ですか。）
- [ ] Do you really think ～ ?
  （本当に～と思うの？）
- [ ] I admit they have some effect, but ～
  （ある効果があることは認めるが、～）
- [ ] regardless of ～
  （～にかかわらず）
- [ ] The result will be the same.
  （結果は同じである。）
- [ ] What do you think?
  （どう思うの？）
- [ ] in addition to ～
  （～に加えて）

◆すぐに使える表現　Possible Opinions

☐ Metal detectors are a last resort.
（金属探知機は、最後の手段である。）

☐ It's schools' responsibility to take any measures possible to protect students.
（生徒を守るために可能な手段を講じるのは、学校の責任である。）

☐ Delinquent students have a tendency to repeat the same mistakes.
（非行生徒は同じ間違いを繰り返す傾向にある。）

☐ Schools should cooperate with police officers.
（学校は警察官と協力すべきである。）

☐ Teachers need to think of students' privacy first.
（教師は生徒のプライバシーをまず考える必要がある。）

ケース 8 男性のメーキャップの是非
Track 8　Men wearing makeup: for or against?

❓ 海水浴での日焼け止めは一般化している。今後、男性のメーク市場はどうなっていくだろうか。

ダイアローグ
Dialogue

TV anchor: According to a survey released on Monday, people **judge** others **based** mainly **on** their appearance. Last year, cosmetics for men **exceeded** sales **expectations**. Men are more **fashion** and brand **conscious** than ever. They buy cosmetics for men such as **hair dyes**, **moisturizers** and so forth. Accordingly, the number of men who wear makeup **is on the rise**.

月曜日に発表された調査によると、人々は他人を主に外見で判断するそうです。
昨年、男性用化粧品が売り上げ予想を上回りました。男性は今まで以上に流行やブランドに関心があります。彼らは、髪染めや保湿剤などの男性用化粧品を購入します。その結果、メークをする男性の数が増えています。

ケース 8　男性のメーキャップの是非

Diana: I think it's difficult to **estimate** the number of men who wear makeup. Do you wear makeup?

メークしている男性の数を推定するのは、難しいわよね。あなたはメークしているの？

John: No, I don't. Do you think it's a good thing?

僕はしていない。男性の化粧は良いことだと思う？

Diana: Yeah, I think it's fine. If they look clean and fresh with their makeup on, that's **acceptable**.

ええ、良いと思うわ。メークしてきれいで清潔に見えれば、それは許容範囲ね。

John: In my case, I use **facial wash** and **apply** moisturizers to make myself look good. It's because I **have terribly dry skin**. But that's all. I don't **consider** those things to be makeup. To sum it up, I oppose the idea of men wearing makeup.

僕の場合には、清潔に見えるように洗顔剤を使い、保湿剤をつけるんだ。僕はひどい乾燥肌だからね。でもそれだけだよ。それらはメークとは思わないけど。要するに男性がメークすることには反対さ。

Diana: I see it as a good thing. Sometimes my friends **look depressed** with **bags under their eyes due to lack of sleep**. But they can make themselves look more **cheerful** with a little makeup. I just want men to **be** more **conscious of** their appearance.

私もそれは良いと思うわ。時々、睡眠不足のせいで目の下に隈ができて元気がないように見える友達がいるの。でも、ちょっとしたメークでもっと元気に見せることができるの。私はただ男性に外見をもっと意識してもらいたいのよ。

John: I'm not saying that **grooming and appearance** aren't important to me. I look into the mirror every morning to check my hair style, **eyebrows** and so on. However, I hate **foundation**, **lipstick**, **eye shadow** and anything else like that. I don't like the feel of makeup

僕は身だしなみが重要でないとは言っていないよ。毎朝鏡を見て、髪型や眉毛などをチェックするんだ。でも、ファウンデーション、口紅、アイシャドウなどは嫌いさ。顔に塗るメークの感覚が好きになれないんだ。

47

on my face.

Diana: Ha-ha, I'm not talking about cosmetics like those. What I mean is that men need to look **neat and tidy**. For example, using **deodorant** to reduce **offensive body odor** and **gel** to **do their hair**. With a little effort, men can **make a much better impression**.

ははは。私はそんな化粧品のことを言っている訳じゃないの。私の言いたいことは、男性が清潔にする必要があること。例えば、不快な体臭を消す体臭防止剤や髪を整えるジェルを使うことよ。ちょっとした努力で男性はかなり良い印象を与えることができるの。

John: Do you mean that men's grooming doesn't necessarily mean wearing makeup but **paying particular attention to** appearance? **In this regard,** I don't oppose what you've said.

君の言う男性の身だしなみって、必ずしもメークをすることじゃなく、外見に特に気をつけることなんだね。この点に関しては、君の意見に反対しないよ。

Words & Phrases

- judge 〜を判断する
- based on 〜 〜に基づいて
- exceed 〜を超える
- expectation 予想、期待
- fashion conscious 流行を気にする
- hair dye 毛髪染料
- moisturizer 肌の保湿剤
- be on the rise 増加している
- estimate 〜を推定する
- acceptable 受け入れることができる
- facial wash 洗顔料
- apply 〜を使う
- have terribly dry skin ひどい乾燥肌である
- consider 〜を…とみなす
- look depressed 落ち込んで見える、憂鬱そうだ
- bags under one's eyes 目の下の隈、たるみ
- due to 〜 〜が原因で
- lack of sleep 睡眠不足
- cheerful 陽気な
- be conscious of 〜 〜を意識している
- grooming and appearance 身だしなみ
- eyebrow 眉毛
- foundation ファンデーション
- lipstick 口紅
- eye shadow アイシャドウ
- neat and tidy きちんと整って
- deodorant 体臭防止剤
- offensive body odor 不快な体臭
- gel ジェル
- do one's hair ヘアスタイルを整える
- make a better impression 良い印象を与える
- pay particular attention to 〜 〜に特別の注意を払う

Tips: よく使われる表現 ―特に異存なし―

- I don't oppose what you've said.
  (あなたが言ったことに反対はしない。)
- I have nothing against what you've just said.
  (あなたが言ったことに対して異存はない。)
- I have no opposition to your opinion.
  (あなたの意見に対して反対しない。)
- I don't oppose your idea.
  (私はあなたの考えに反対しない。)

◆ その他の表現

- [ ] according to a survey released on Monday
  (月曜日に発表されたある調査によると)
- [ ] accordingly （その結果、それで）
- [ ] in one's case （〜の場合）
- [ ] to sum it up （結論として、要するに）
- [ ] I oppose the idea of men wearing makeup.
  （男性がメークする考えには反対です。）
- [ ] what I mean is that 〜 （私が言いたいことは〜である）
- [ ] in this regard （この点について）

◆ すぐに使える表現　Possible Opinions

- [ ] Makeup seems to be distracting.
  （メークすると、気が散るように思える。）
- [ ] It's not good to judge people by appearances.
  （外見で人々を判断するのは良くない。）
- [ ] Don't be fooled by appearances.
  （外見に惑わされるな。）
- [ ] Everybody likes to feel attractive.
  （誰もが自分は魅力的だと思いたい。）
- [ ] Wearing makeup is time- and money-consuming.
  （メークをするには時間とお金がかかる。）
- [ ] Men recognize it's important to be fit and look good to succeed in business.
  （男性はビジネスで成功するためには、健康で見栄え良く見えることが重要だと認識している。）

ケース9 校内スマホ禁止の是非

Track 9　Banning smartphones in school: for or against?

未成年のスマホを巡るトラブルが後を絶たない。スマホの校内禁止は必要なのだろうか。

ダイアローグ
Dialogue

TV Anchor: Recently, **web-related crimes** involving **minors** have **been on the rise**. As a result, the local government **issued a** special **notice** that bans students in primary and middle schools from bringing smartphones to school. This is because smartphones make it possible for students to **access** websites with **harmful content** too easily.

最近、未成年を巻き込んだウェブ関連の犯罪が増えてきています。結果として、地方自治体が小学生と中学生の学校へのスマホの持ち込みを禁止する特別の通知を出しました。これは、スマホを使うと、生徒が有害コンテンツを含むウェブサイトにあまりにも簡単にアクセスすることが可能だからです。

Diana:	Do you agree with the government's move to ban smartphones in school?	学校でのスマホを禁止する自治体の動きに賛成ですか。
John:	No, I don't. Smartphones are not only convenient; they're a **must in this day and age**. **Wherever I am**, I can talk with my friends. They are especially useful when I get lost or I am late. Smartphones are **absolutely** necessary. Students feel the same, I think.	いや。スマホは便利なだけじゃない。今日では、スマホは必需品だよ。どこにいても友人と話せるし。スマホは特に迷子になった時や遅れる時には役に立つよね。スマホは絶対に必要だよ。生徒も同じだと思うよ。
Diana:	I agree with you. However, it's true students can easily access websites with harmful content. Besides, they tend to spend a lot of time playing games on their smartphones. It costs a lot of money and is **time-consuming**.	あなたに賛成よ。でも、生徒が有害コンテンツを含むウェブサイトにたやすくアクセスできるのは本当ね。それに生徒はスマホでゲームをして長い時間を過ごす傾向にあるわ。たくさんお金がかかるし時間の浪費ね。
John:	True, but smartphones allow them to do helpful things such as send and receive e-mail, take pictures, and watch videos, too. They are really **amazing**.	そうだね。でも、スマホのおかげで、私たちがメールを送受信したり、写真を撮ったり、ビデオを見たりするなど役に立つこともできるよ。スマホは本当にすごいよ。
Diana:	Yes, however, they not only have those functions, but, as I **implied** before, can also function as **toys**. For instance, students can play games, **surf the web** and listen to music as well. **In a sense**, bringing smartphones to school is the same as bringing toys to school.	そうね。でも、スマホはそういう機能だけじゃなくて、先にほのめかしたように、オモチャとしての機能もあるわ。例えば、ゲームはできるし、ネットサーフィンできるし、音楽も聴けるわ。ある意味、学校にスマホを持ち込むことは学校にオモチャを持ち込むことと同じよ。
John:	You're right. How about allowing them to	そうだね。生徒にスマホ

bring smartphones to school, but only those with **limited** functions? Students must learn the **appropriate time and place** to use smartphones.

の学校への持ち込みを許すのはどうかな、でも限られた機能つきでね。生徒はスマホを使う適切な時間と場所を学ばなければいけないよ。

Diana: Yeah. You have a good point.

そうね。それも一理あるわ。

John: In any case, students need to learn how to use smartphones **responsibly** before they become **adults**.

いずれにしても、生徒は大人になる前にスマホの責任ある使い方を身につける必要があるね。

Words & Phrases

- web-related　ウェブ関連の
- crime　犯罪
- minor　未成年者
- be on the rise　増加している
- issue a notice　通知を発する
- access　〜にアクセスする、〜に接続する
- harmful content　有害コンテンツ、有害な内容
- must　不可欠なもの
- in this day and age　今日では、現代では
- wherever I am　どこにいても
- absolutely　絶対に、完全に
- time-consuming　時間のかかる
- amazing　びっくりさせるような
- imply　〜をほのめかす、〜を暗に示す
- toy　おもちゃ
- surf the web　ネットサーフィンする
- in a sense　ある意味では
- limited　限られた
- appropriate time and place　適切な時間と場所
- responsibly　責任をもって
- adult　大人

Tips よく使われる表現―状況・場合―

☐ in any case
　（ともかく、いずれにしても）

☐ at any rate
　（ともかく、いずれにしても）

☐ anyway
　（ともかく、いずれにしても）

◆その他の表現

☐ as a result
　（結果として）

☐ Do you agree with the ～ 's move?
　（～の動きに賛成するの？）

☐ Students feel the same.
　（生徒も同意見である。）

☐ I agree with you.
　（あなたに賛成である。）

☐ besides
　（さらに）

☐ You have a good point.
　（良いところをついている。）

◆すぐに使える表現　Possible Opinions

- [ ] It's necessary to block children's access to websites containing harmful content.
（有害コンテンツを含むウェブサイトへ子どもたちのアクセスを遮断する必要がある。）

- [ ] It's better to install parental controls on students' smartphones until they become high school students.
（高校生になるまでは生徒のスマホにはフィルタリング機能をインストールするのが良い。）

- [ ] It's better to let students pay their own smartphone bills.
（スマホの請求は生徒に払わせるのが良い。）

- [ ] It's not easy to find public phones in an emergency.
（緊急時に公衆電話を見つけるのは容易ではない。）

- [ ] A smartphone ringing in the middle of class can be disruptive.
（スマホが授業中に突然鳴り出すと迷惑である。）

- [ ] Most smartphones include a GPS transmitter that traces location. Smartphones that have been lost can easily be located with GPS.
（ほとんどのスマホには位置を知らせるGPSの発信機がついている。なくしたスマホはGPSでその位置がわかるので便利である。）

ケース 10 電車内優先席の是非
Track 10   Priority seats on trains: for or against?

⁉ 電車内の優先席を巡って様々な意見がある。電車内の優先席は必要なのだろうか。

ダイアローグ
Dialogue

TV anchor: In Japan, most train cars have **priority seats** for **the elderly**, **physically disabled** and pregnant women. However, not many people give up their priority seat to someone who **actually** needs it. There is a **discussion** as to whether or not we should change all seats on trains into priority seats.

日本では、ほとんどの電車に高齢者、身障者や妊婦のための優先席があります。しかし、実際に優先席を必要とする人々に優先席を譲る人は多くありません。電車のすべての席を優先席に変えるべきかどうかについて、議論されています。

John: What do you think about this issue?

この問題についてどう思う?

ケース10　電車内優先席の是非

Diana: As far as I'm concerned, it's a good idea. If we change the system itself, most physically disabled people as well as the elderly and the **pregnant** will be able to find a seat on the train.

私としては、それは良い考えだと思うわ。もしシステムそのものを変えれば、高齢者や妊婦だけでなく、ほとんどの身障者が電車で座ることができるようになるわ。

John: Isn't it difficult to tell who is physically disabled? For example, people who wear **artificial legs** may look healthy, but, actually, they really need priority seats. How do you tell such people **apart from** others?

身障者を見分けるのって難しくないかな？例えば、義足をつけている人は健康に見えるかもしれないけど、実際には優先席を本当に必要としているよ。そのような人をどうやって他の人と見分けるんだい？

Diana: Well, how about elderly people? It's quite easy to tell who is old.

それじゃ高齢の人はどう？誰が高齢かかなり見分けやすいわ。

John: No, it's not that easy. Sometimes it's difficult to tell who is elderly or not **by appearance**. Once I tried to give a priority seat to someone who seemed old and he suddenly got angry. He looked old, but actually he was not.

それ程簡単じゃないよ。時々、高齢かどうか外見で見分けるのは難しいよ。一度高齢に見える人に優先席を譲ろうとしたんだ。その人が突然怒ってさ。彼は高齢に見えたけど、実際にはそうじゃなかったんだ。

Diana: Yeah. **In fact**, I had a **similar** experience. What should we do to solve this issue?

そうね。実際、私も同じような経験をしたことがあるの。この問題を解決するために、何をすべきかしら。

John: **Passengers** with poor **manners** won't **give up** their seats **even if** the system is changed. What do you think?

たとえシステムが変わっても、マナーが悪い乗客は自分の席を譲ろうとしないんだ。どう思う？

Diana: Well then, a top priority in solving this issue

そうね、この問題を解決

would be improving passengers' manners **rather than** increasing the number of priority seats. | するために最も重要なことは、優先席の数を増やすことより乗客のマナーを変えることじゃないかしら。

Words & Phrases

- priority seat　優先席
- the elderly　高齢者
- the physically disabled　身障者
- actually　実際に
- discussion　議論
- pregnant　妊娠している
- artificial leg　義足
- apart from 〜　〜は別として、〜はさておき
- by appearance　外見で
- in fact　実際には
- similar　よく似た
- passenger　乗客
- manner　マナー
- give up 〜　〜を譲る
- even if 〜　たとえ〜でも
- … rather than 〜　〜よりむしろ…

ケース10　電車内優先席の是非

Tips よく使われる表現—観点①—

☐ as far as I'm concerned
（私としては）
☐ for my part
（私としては）
☐ as for me
（私に関しては）
☐ speaking for myself
（私について言えば）
☐ personally
（個人的には）
☐ in my book
（私の考えでは）

◆その他の表現

☐ There is a discussion as to whether or not we should 〜.
（私たちが〜すべきかどうかということについて一つの議論がある。）
☐ What do you think about this issue?
（この問題についてどう思う？）
☐ What do you think?
（どう思うの？）
☐ a top priority is 〜
（最優先課題は〜である）

◆すぐに使える表現　Possible Opinions

- [ ] Some young people pretend to sleep on the train.
  （電車で寝たふりをする若者がいる。）
- [ ] Everyone pays the same train fare. Why should we have to give up our seats?
  （みんな同じ電車料金を払っている。なぜ席を譲らなきゃいけないの？）
- [ ] It's difficult to improve manners.
  （マナーを改善することは難しい。）
- [ ] Young people who are sitting in priority seats should give up their seats to elderly people who are standing.
  （優先席に座っている若者は、立っているお年寄りに席を譲るべきである。）

ケース 11 暴力描写の多いテレビゲームの是非
Track 11   Violent video games: for or against?

近年、青少年の凶悪犯罪が増加傾向にある。暴力描写の多い映画やゲームは犯罪と関係があるのだろうか。

ダイアローグ
Dialogue

TV anchor: A 17-year-old boy was **arrested on suspicion of** killing his teacher. He was said to be a video game **enthusiast**. He liked to kill **zombies** with guns and **swords** in video games.

17歳の少年が先生を殺した容疑で逮捕されました。彼はテレビゲームの熱狂的ファンだったと言われていました。彼はテレビゲームの中では銃や刀でゾンビを殺すのを好んでいました。

John: **Murder** again?

また殺人なの？

Diana: Yeah. The news said he **is obsessed with** violent video games.

そうよ。ニュースによれば、彼は暴力描写の多いテレビゲームに取りつかれていたそうね。

John: That's **terrifying**. When he killed his teacher, he couldn't **tell fantasy from reality**. I think there is a **close relationship** between **juvenile crimes** and playing violent video games.

それは恐ろしいね。彼が先生を殺した時、彼は幻想と現実が区別できなかったんだ。青少年犯罪と暴力描写の多いテレビゲームをすることとの間に密接な関係があると思うね。

Diana: Maybe. So you mean you agree with the movement to **restrict** the sales of violent video games?

おそらくね。それじゃ、あなたは暴力描写の多いテレビゲームの販売を制限する動きには賛成だということなの？

John: Yeah, I do. I'm 100% sure such games have a **negative effect** on young people. In fact, some local governments in Japan have decided to introduce restrictions on violent video games. For example, people younger than 18 can't buy such games in those **prefectures**.

うん。そういう類のゲームは若者に悪影響を及ぼしていると100%確信しているよ。実際に、日本のいくつかの地方自治体は暴力描写の多いテレビゲームに対する規制を導入することに決めたしね。例えば、18歳以下の若者はそれらの県ではそのようなゲームは買えないんだ。

Diana: I don't agree with you because the relationship between juvenile crimes and violent video games has not yet been **scientifically proven**. Also, it's very difficult to define just how violent such video games are.

私はあなたに賛成しないわ。なぜなら青少年犯罪と暴力描写の多いテレビゲームとの間の関係が科学的に証明された訳じゃないもの。それに、テレビゲームが、どれ程暴力描写が多いかを定義するのはとても難しいわ。

John: It may be very difficult to **define** how violent video games are, but still, it's better to do something about it rather than to do nothing at all. That's why I **admire** the decision of those **local governments** to restrict the sales of violent video games. They **recognize** a

テレビゲームが、どれ程暴力的かを定義するのはとても難しいかもしれないけど、それでもまったく何もしないよりは、何かした方が良いんだ。だから、暴力描写が多いテレビゲームの販売を規制する地方自治体の決断を賞賛しているんだ。彼らは青少年犯罪とそれらの

possible relationship between juvenile crimes and such games. | ゲームとの間に関係があるかもしれないことを認識しているんだ。

Words & Phrases

- arrest　〜を逮捕する
- on suspicion of 〜　〜の容疑で
- enthusiast　熱狂者、熱中している人
- zombie　ゾンビ
- sword　剣
- murder　殺人
- be obsessed with 〜　〜に取りつかれている、〜に夢中である
- terrifying　恐ろしい
- tell fantasy from reality　空想と現実を区別する
- close relationship　親しい間柄
- juvenile crime　少年犯罪
- restrict　〜を制限する、〜を限定する
- negative effect　悪影響、マイナス効果
- prefecture　県
- scientifically proven　科学的に証明された
- define　〜を定義する
- admire　〜を称賛する
- local government　地方自治体
- recognize　〜と認める、〜だとわかる

Tips　よく使われる表現―強調②―

☐ in fact
　（実際には）
☐ the reality is that ～
　（実は～である）
☐ as a matter of fact
　（実を言うと）
☐ in reality
　（実際には）

◆その他の表現

☐ there is a close relationship between ～ and …
　（～と…との間に密接な関係がある）
☐ So you mean you agree with ～ ?
　（つまり～に賛成だということなの？）
☐ I'm 100% sure such games have a negative effect on young people.
　（そのようなゲームは若者に悪い影響を与えると 100% 確信している。）
☐ for example
　（例えば）
☐ I don't agree with you because ～
　（～の理由であなたに賛成しない）
☐ that's why ～
　（そういう訳で～である）

ケース11　暴力描写の多いテレビゲームの是非

◆すぐに使える表現　Possible Opinions

- It might lead to restrictions on freedom of speech.
  （表現の自由の制限につながるかもしれない。）
- Young people should have the right to play violent video games for fun.
  （若者は暴力描写の多いテレビゲームを楽しむ権利を持つべきである。）
- Playing violent games is the same as watching violent TV shows.
  （暴力描写の多いゲームをすることは、暴力描写の多いテレビショーを見ることと同じである。）
- The name of the game concerning this issue is definitely prevention.
  （この問題について肝心なのは、間違いなく予防することである。）
- Young people who can't discern reality from fantasy are prone to crime regardless of video games.
  （現実と幻想とを区別できない若者は、テレビゲームの内容にかかわらず、罪を犯す傾向にある。）

ケース 12　未成年者の門限の是非
Track 12
Curfews for minors: for or against?

門限は親と子供との家庭内のルールである。門限は何歳まで必要なのだろうか。

ダイアローグ
Dialogue

TV anchor: A lot of junior high students **are involved in** crimes at night. After **a series of sex-related crimes**, one governor proposed making a **curfew** a **local government ordinance**.

大勢の中学生が夜間に犯罪に巻き込まれています。一連の性犯罪の後、一人の知事が門限を地方条例で設置するという提案をしました。

John: Did you have a curfew when you were in junior high?

君が中学生の時、門限があったかい？

Diana: Yes, I did. Nine **o'clock, sharp**.

ええ。9時ちょうどね。

ケース12　未成年者の門限の是非

John: Did you ever return home after curfew?

門限に遅れたことはあったの？

Diana: Yes, sometimes I did. Then I would phone my mom to get her **permission** to come home late. It was really **annoying** to have to call. How about you?

ええ、時々ね。その時は、遅く帰る許可をとるために、母に電話をしたものよ。電話しなければならないというのは本当に煩わしかったわ。あなたはどうなの。

John: As for me, I didn't have a **fixed curfew**. I just learned to **make it a rule to** come home before dinner. My family **regards** having dinner together **as** very important. In fact, it was always really fun to talk with my family during dinnertime. My parents definitely taught me the importance of family over rules. Did you try to change the time of your curfew?

僕はと言えば、決まった門限はなかったね。僕は、ただ夕食前に家に帰るようになったんだ。僕の家族は夕食を一緒にとることをとても大切にしているんだ。実際、夕食時に家族と話すのはいつも本当に楽しかったよ。両親は、規則以上に家族の大切さを教えてくれたことは確かだね。君は、門限の時間を変えようとしたことはあるのかい？

Diana: Yes, I did. My parents asked me to **explain the reason every time** I wanted to change my curfew. **Thanks to** them, I learned how to **negotiate**.

ええ、あるわ。私の両親は私が門限を変えようとする度に、その理由を説明するよう求めたわ。両親のおかげで、私は交渉する方法を身につけたの。

John: So your **negotiation skills** were **cultivated** by your parents. Probably they wanted you to learn how to negotiate naturally through such a conversation.

君の交渉術は両親によって育まれたんだね。おそらく君の両親は、夕食時の会話をとおして自然に交渉する術を君に身につけて欲しかったんだね。

Diana: You know, I didn't even realize that! If true, I should take the time to **appreciate** what my

私はそのことに気づきさえしなかったわ。もし本当なら、時間をとって両

67

parents did to **improve** my negotiation skills. But, even at 23, I still have a curfew. I can't believe it! What do you think?

親が私の交渉術を向上させるためにしてくれたことに感謝したいわ。でも23歳になっても、まだ門限があるのよ。信じられないわ。どう思う？

Words & Phrases

- be involved in ～　～に関わる、～に巻き込まれる
- a series of ～　一連の～
- sex-related crime　性犯罪
- curfew　門限；(夜間)外出禁止令
- local government ordinance　地方条例
- (at)～o'clock, sharp　～時ぴったりに
- permission　許可
- annoying　うっとうしい、気に障る
- fixed curfew　決められた門限
- make it a rule to ～　～するのを常とする
- regard ～ as …　～を…とみなす
- explain the reason　理由を説明する
- every time　毎回～するたびに
- thanks to ～　～のおかげで
- negotiate　(～について)交渉する、協定する
- negotiation skill　交渉術
- cultivate　～を育てる、～を耕す
- appreciate　～を感謝する、～を正しく評価する
- improve　～を向上させる、～を高める

Tips よく使われる表現—強調③—

- definitely
  (当然)
- certainly
  (確かに)
- without a doubt
  (疑いなく)
- There's no doubt about it.
  (それには疑いの余地がない。)
- there is little doubt that ～
  (～は疑いの余地がほとんどない)
- I can say for sure that ～
  (はっきり言えることは～)
- there's no question that ～
  (～に関しては疑いの余地がない)

◆その他の表現

- How about you?
  (あなたはどうなの？)
- as for me
  (私としては、私の場合)
- I didn't even realize that.
  (それは知らなかった。)
- What do you think?
  (どう思うの？)

◆すぐに使える表現　Possible Opinions

☐ A curfew may hinder children over 15 years old from becoming independent.
（門限のせいで、15歳以上の子供たちが自立するのを妨げるかもしれない。）

☐ People younger than 15 learn a sense of responsibility.
（15歳以下の若者は責任感を学ぶ。）

☐ A curfew could be a good way to teach younger people negotiation skills.
（門限は若者に交渉術を教える良い方法になりうる。）

☐ Curfews for teens may create poor relationships between parents and children if the children don't understand the importance of the curfews themselves.
（子どもたちがその重要性を理解していなければ、10代の門限は、親と子どもの人間関係を悪くするかもしれない。）

ケース 13 選挙権年齢の引き下げの是非

Track 13　Lowering the voting age: for or against?

一般的に若年齢層の人々の投票率が低い。そのような状況で選挙権年齢を引き下げることは必要なのだろうか。

ダイアローグ
Dialogue

TV anchor: **Society** is changing **rapidly**. The government should listen more to young people's **opinions**. In this regard, it's better to lower the voting age from 20 to 18 **in order to facilitate** a change in the government through the power of young people. This change will then bring **social reforms** and lead society **in a good direction**.

社会は急速に変化しています。政府はもっと若者の意見に耳を傾けるべきです。この点で、若者の力で政治における変化を促進するために20歳から18歳に選挙権年齢を引き下げれば良いのです。そうすればこの変更が社会改革をもたらし、社会を良い方向に導いていくでしょう。

Diana: **It's time for** Japan **to** lower the voting age from 20 to 18. 18-year-olds are old **enough to** have adult **privileges** and **responsibilities**, especially the right to vote. Then young people can join in politics as voters.

日本は選挙権年齢を20歳から18歳に引き下げる時期よね。18歳の若者は大人の権利と責任を持っても良い年齢でしょう。特に選挙権に関しては。そうすれば、若者が有権者として政治に参加できるわ。

John: I don't think so. Young people **nowadays give little thought to** important **political issues** because they spend most of their time reading **comics** and playing video games.

僕はそう思わないよ。最近の若者は重要な政治問題にほとんど関心を持たないじゃない。彼らは、ほとんどの時間を漫画やテレビゲームをして過ごしているしね。

Diana: That's true, but there are **a large number of** older adults who act the same way. If younger people are given the chance to vote, they may think about **politics** more. **Candidates** would also have to think of a campaign **message** not only for adults over 20, but for voters under 20 as well. That means they are likely to **become** more **aware of** young people's opinions.

それは事実だけど、同じように行動する大人もたくさんいるわよ。もし若者が投票する機会を与えられれば、もっと政治について考えるかもしれないわ。それに候補者は、20歳以上の成人のためだけでなく、20歳以下の有権者のためにも選挙運動のメッセージを考えなくてはならないのよ。つまり候補者はもっと若者の意見を意識するようになるわ。

John: I still don't agree. If 18-year-olds are allowed to vote, then they **are regarded as** full adults. If that's the case, does that mean they will also be allowed to drink and smoke? I'm afraid they will **waste** their parents' money on alcohol and cigarettes.

僕はまだ賛成できないよ。18歳の若者に投票することが認められたら、彼らは完全に大人として認められることになるんだよ。もしそうだとしたら、お酒を飲んだりタバコを吸ったりすることが許されるってこと？彼らはお酒やタバコに親のお金を浪費することにならないかな。

Diana: I understand your point. But don't you think

あなたの言いたいことは

the Japanese in general will become more interested in politics if young people are regarded as responsible adults and allowed to vote?

わかるわ。でも、もし若者が責任ある大人として見なされ投票することが許されれば、一般的に日本人が政治に対してもっと関心を持つようになると思わない？

John: I don't think so. It isn't **a matter of** their age, but a matter of their **maturity**. 18-year-olds are just too **childish** to become politically involved.

僕はそうは思わないね。それは年齢の問題ではなく、成熟度の問題なんだ。18歳の若者は、子供っぽ過ぎて、政治には参加できないよ。

Words & Phrases

- society　社会
- rapidly　急速に
- opinion　意見
- in order to ～　～するために
- facilitate　～を促進する
- social reform　社会変革
- in a good direction　良い方向に
- it's time for … to ～　…が～する時です
- … enough to ～　～するのに十分な…
- privilege　特権
- responsibility　責任、義務
- nowadays　最近は
- give little thought to ～　～にあまり関心を持たない
- political issue　政治的課題
- comic　漫画
- a large number of ～　多くの～
- politics　政治、政策
- candidate　候補者
- message　メッセージ、声明
- become aware of ～　～に気づく、～を知るようになる
- be regarded as ～　～として見なされる
- waste　～を浪費する、～をムダにする
- a matter of ～　～の問題
- maturity　成熟度、十分な成果
- childish　子供の、子供じみた

> **Tips** よく使われる表現―逆接①―

- [ ] that's true, but 〜
    （それは本当だが、〜）
- [ ] but the fact remains that…
    （しかし、実際は…）
- [ ] indeed…, but 〜
    （実は…、しかし〜）
- [ ] contrary to one's expectation
    （期待に反して）
- [ ] contrary to predictions
    （予測に反して）

◆その他の表現

- [ ] I don't think so.
    （私はそう思わない。）
- [ ] I still don't agree.
    （まだ賛成しない。）
- [ ] if that's the case, 〜
    （もしそうだとしたら〜）
- [ ] I understand your point.
    （あなたの言いたいことはわかる。）
- [ ] in this regard
    （この点で）

◆すぐに使える表現　Possible Opinions

☐ 18-year-olds will build a more attractive society.
（18歳の若者はより魅力的な社会を築くだろう。）

☐ It's the responsibility of young people to make the future of Japan brighter.
（日本の未来を明るくするのは若者の責任である。）

☐ 18-year-olds are not interested in politics. They read few books or newspapers.
（18歳の若者は、政治に関心がない。彼らは本や新聞をほとんど読まない。）

☐ 18-year-olds aren't mature enough to select the best candidate.
（18歳の若者は、最高の候補者を選べるほど成熟していない。）

☐ Elected officials make decisions that directly affect our lives.
（選出議員の決定は、私たちの生活に直接影響を及ぼす。）

☐ The voting age in many countries is 18, so we should lower the voting age in Japan.
（多くの国で選挙権年齢が18歳である。そのため、日本でも選挙権年齢を引き下げるべきである。）

ケース 14 患者へのガン告知の是非

Track 14　Informing patients of cancer diagnoses: for or against?

患者へのガン告知の是非が論じられている。患者が質の高い人生を過ごすためには、どうすればよいのだろうか。

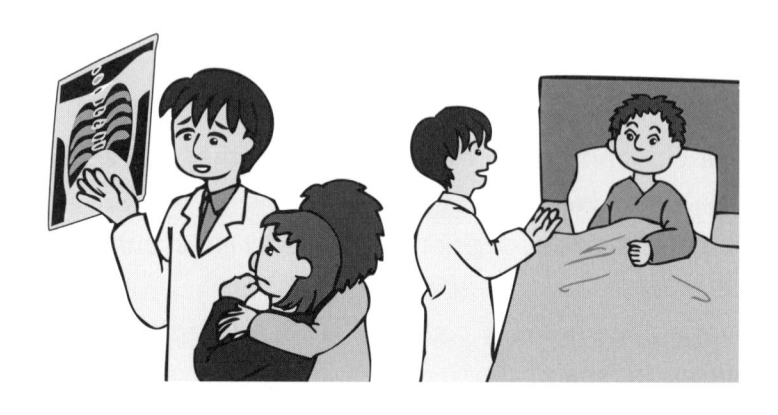

ダイアローグ
Dialogue

TV anchor: Before 1981, **stroke** was the most **common cause** of death in Japan. Owing to a **westernized diet** and lifestyle, **cancer replaced** stroke **as** the No. 1 killer in only a few **decades**. In Japan, the **ratio** of patients **informed of** a cancer **diagnosis** before their family is **by far** lower than that of the US.

1981年以前は、日本では、脳卒中が最も多い死因でした。西洋式の食事やライフスタイルのせいで、ほんの数十年でガンが一番の死因として取って代わりました。日本では、家族より前に患者がガンの告知を受けた割合がアメリカ合衆国のそれよりかなり低くなっています。

John: Is it **common** to let a patient's family know

まず患者の家族へのガン

ケース14　患者へのガン告知の是非

about a cancer diagnosis first?

診断の告知が一般的なの？

Diana: Yeah, especially with **minors** who are not **mature** enough to understand the fact that they have cancer. So, parents **judge whether** their children are able to handle knowing it **or not**.

ええ、特に自分がガンを患っている事実を理解するのに十分成長していない未成年者にはね。だから、子供がその事実を知って受けとめ、対処できるかどうか両親が判断するの。

John: Would you want to be informed of cancer first?

君はガンの告知を最初にされたいかい？

Diana: No. I'm sure I'd **get depressed** if I knew I was going to die soon.

いいえ。もし、すぐ死ぬとわかれば、きっと精神的に落ち込んでしまうわ。

John: Diana, you're misunderstanding something. In the past, cancer was **infamous** as an **incurable disease**. Today, however, cancer has become a **treatable** or **controllable** disease.

ダイアナ、君は何か誤解しているよ。昔は、ガンは不治の病として悪名高かった。でも、今日では、ガンは治療可能か管理可能な病気になっているんだ。

Diana: I didn't know that.

それは知らなかったわ。

John: According to a recent survey, the ratio of patients directly informed of cancer has increased because cancer itself is no longer an incurable, untreatable disease. Besides, **even if** patients might have only one year to live, I'm sure they would want to **make the most of** every minute.

ある最近の調査によると、ガンはもはや不治の病や治療不可能な病ではないので、患者に直接ガンの告知をする割合が増えたそうだよ。しかも、たとえ、患者が一年しか生きられなくても、きっと患者は一瞬一瞬を思い切り楽しみたいはずだよ。

Diana: I understand that, but if some patients know they have cancer, they may lose hope and convince themselves that they will die. No one knows for sure if patients will **beat** cancer or not.

それは、わかったわ、でも、もし何人かの患者の中にはガンを患っているとわかれば、希望を失い自分は死ぬと思い込んでしまう人がいるかもしれないわ。患者がガンに打ち勝つかどうかは、誰にも確かなことはわからないもの。

Words & Phrases

- ☐ stroke　脳卒中、発作
- ☐ common cause　一般的原因、共通の利害
- ☐ westernized diet　西洋式の食事
- ☐ cancer　ガン
- ☐ replace ~ as …　~を…としてとってかわる
- ☐ decade　10年間
- ☐ ratio　割合、比率
- ☐ be informed of ~　~について知らされる
- ☐ diagnosis　診断
- ☐ by far　（比較、最上級を強めて）はるかに、非常に
- ☐ common　一般的な、共通な
- ☐ minor　未成年者
- ☐ mature　成熟する
- ☐ judge　~を判断する、~を評価する
- ☐ whether ~ or not　~かどうか
- ☐ get depressed　落ち込む、気がめいる
- ☐ infamous　悪名高い
- ☐ incurable disease　不治の病
- ☐ treatable　治療可能な
- ☐ controllable　管理可能な
- ☐ even if ~　たとえ~だとしても
- ☐ make the most of ~　~を最大限に活用する
- ☐ beat　~を克服する、~に打ち勝つ

ケース14　患者へのガン告知の是非

Tips　よく使われる表現—誤解—

- ☐ You misunderstand something.
  （あなたは何か誤解している。）
- ☐ You've got me wrong.
  （私を誤解している。）
- ☐ Don't get me wrong.
  （誤解しないで！）
- ☐ You have me all wrong.
  （ひどい誤解である。）
- ☐ You misunderstand me.
  （あなたは私を誤解している。）
- ☐ It's a big misunderstanding.
  （それは大きな誤解である。）
- ☐ You and I got our wires crossed.
  （あなたと私とで行き違いがあった。）

◆その他の表現

- ☐ owing to ～
  （～のおかげで、せいで）
- ☐ I didn't know that.
  （それは知らなかった。）
- ☐ according to a recent survey
  （最近のある調査によると）
- ☐ I understand that, but ～
  （それは理解するけど、～）

◆すぐに使える表現　Possible Opinions

- [ ] Patients are overwhelmed by despair rather than fear.
（患者は恐怖というより、むしろ失望に打ちのめされてしまう。）
- [ ] Instead of telling child patients with frightening words, you can tell them "Your blood factory isn't working."
（恐ろしい言葉で子供の患者に言う代わりに、血液工場がうまく機能していないと言えばよい。）
- [ ] Patients need follow-up treatment after the diagnosis.
（患者は診断の後、追加治療が必要である。）
- [ ] No one escapes from death, so we must all accept the fact of death.
（誰も死から逃れられない。だから、私たちは死の事実を受け止めなければいけない。）
- [ ] People should be told the fact about how long life will last.
（人々は、残された寿命がどれくらいかという事実について告げられるべきである。）
- [ ] Even if patients have six months to live, they want to know when they will die because they want to make the most of the time they have left.
（たとえ患者があと6カ月しか生きられなくとも、彼らは残された時間を有効に使うためにいつ死ぬかを知りたい。）

ケース15 小学1年生の通塾の是非

Track 15　Primary school first graders going to cram school: for or against?

教育環境を取り巻くさまざまな影響により、小学低学年の通塾率が年々高くなっている。小学1年生にとって通塾は必要なのだろうか。

ダイアローグ
Dialogue

TV anchor: **Cram school** has **played an important role in improving** students' **academic abilities**. **These days**, even **primary school first graders** are being sent to cram school.

生徒の学力を向上させるために、塾は重要な役割を果たしてきています。最近は、小学1年生でさえ塾に通わされています。

John: I think first grade is too young to send children to cram school. Why do parents want to send their children to cram school?

僕は小学1学年の子供を塾に通わせるには幼すぎると思うな。どうして両親は子供を塾へ通わせたいんだろう。

Diana: It's simple. Parents want their children to **get better grades**.

簡単よ。両親は子供たちに良い成績を取ってもらいたいのよ。

John: The textbooks are not that difficult in first grade, so they don't have to go to cram school. Besides, there are many other important things that children should learn **inside and outside of** school.

1年生の教科書はそれ程難しくないよ。だから1年生は塾に行く必要がないよ。それに、学校の中や外には子供たちが他に学ぶべき重要なことがたくさんあるよ。

Diana: **Like what?**

例えばどんなこと？

John: For their health, children must play sports. Through sports, they must learn to **communicate with** others.

健康のため、子供たちはスポーツをする必要があるよ。スポーツをとおして他人とのコミュニケーションのとり方を身につけるんだ。

Diana: **No way!** Children should be able to decide **for themselves** whether they go to cram school or play sports.

まさか。子供たちが塾に通うか、スポーツをするかは子供たちが自分で決めるべきだわ。

John: I don't think so. Some children can't decide **by themselves**. I mean they can't **evaluate** their own academic abilities or decide what they want to do. They need some **advice**.

僕はそう思わないよ。自分で決められない子供だっているさ。つまり子供たちには自分の学力を判断できないし、自分がしたいことを決めることもできないよ。子供たちには、アドバイスが必要だよ。

Diana: Well, you could say that, but both parents and children need to **take time** to talk with **each other** about the merits and demerits of cram school.

そうね、そうともいえるけど、両親と子供たち両者が、塾のメリットとデメリットについてお互い話し合う時間をとる必要がありそうね。

ケース15　小学1年生の通塾の是非

Words & Phrases

- cram school　塾
- play an important role in ～　～で重要な役割を果たす
- improve　～を改善する
- academic ability　学力
- these days　この頃、最近
- primary school　小学校
- first grader　1年生
- get better grades　より良い成績を収める
- inside and outside of　～の内外で
- Like what?　例えばどんなことですか。
- communicate with ～　～とコミュニケーションをとる
- No way!　まさか、そんなことは絶対にあり得ない
- for oneself　自力で、自分のために
- by oneself　独力で、ひとりぼっちで
- evaluate　～を判断する
- advice　助言、アドバイス
- take time　時間をとる
- each other　お互いに

Tips　よく使われる表現—ためらい①—

- you could say that, but ～
  (そうとも言えるけど、～)
- what you said may be true, but ～
  (あなたが言ったことは正しいかもしれない、でも～)
- that may be true, but ～
  (それは正しいかもしれない、でも～)

◆その他の表現

- besides
  (さらに、その上)
- I don't think so.
  (私はそうは思わない。)
- I mean ～　(つまり～)
- talk about the merits and demerits of ～
  (～のメリットとデメリットについて話す)

◆ すぐに使える表現　Possible Opinions

- [ ] It's too early for first graders in primary school to go to cram school.
（小学1年生が塾へ通うのは早すぎる。）
- [ ] It's time- and money- consuming to go to cram school.
（塾へ通うには時間とお金がかかる。）
- [ ] Children are only studying for tests.
（子供たちはテストのためだけに勉強をしている。）
- [ ] Children come to have a passive attitude toward learning if they are forced to learn at cram school.
（もし子供たちが塾で無理に覚えさせられたら、学習に消極的な態度をとるようになる。）
- [ ] Children today have less free time than previous generations. I mean, they don't spend time playing outside with their friends so often.
（今日の子供たちは、前の世代よりも自由時間が少ない。つまり、友達と外で過ごす時間があまりない。）

ケース 16　ダイエットの是非

Track 16

Going on a diet: for or against?

> 一般的に太り過ぎは健康に良くないという。美的欲求から痩せるダイエットは必要なのだろうか。

ダイアローグ / Dialogue

TV anchor: More and more children are **getting skinnier**. Nowadays, they **pay too much attention to** their looks. **Pop stars and models** in magazines are usually **thin**. Moreover, fat people often **get teased** on TV. That's why children want to **lose weight** even when they don't need to.

ますます多くの子供たちが、スリムになっています。最近彼らは外見に注意を払いすぎです。ポップスターや雑誌モデルは、普通やせています。さらに太った人は、テレビでしばしばからかわれます。それで子供たちは必要ない時でさえ減量したがります。

John: Have you ever tried **dieting** before?

以前ダイエットしたことあるかい？

Diana: Many times. I have tried diet food, **dietary supplements** and so on. I don't remember them all.

何回もね。ダイエットフード、ダイエットサプリなどね。全部は覚えてないわよ。

John: So you support the idea of dieting?

ダイエットすることに賛成なの？

Diana: Yes, I support dieting. It's a good way to lose weight. I want to become skinnier than I am now. Then, I think I will look more beautiful. I need to lose 10 more kilograms.

うん、ダイエットを支持するわよ。減量するための1つの良い方法でしょう。今よりは痩せたいもの。そうすれば、もっと美しく見えると思うわ。あと10kg減量の必要があるの。

John: If you **go on a diet** only for that **purpose**, you should stop it **immediately**. Last year in Brazil, a model **died of** losing too much weight. Although she was 174 **centimeters** tall, she **weighed** only 40 kilograms when she died. Being a model is very unhealthy in a sense.

もし痩せる目的のためだけにダイエットするなら、今すぐやめるべきだよ。去年ブラジルで、1人のモデルが減量のし過ぎで亡くなったんだ。彼女は身長が174cmあったけれど、亡くなった時にはわずか40kgしか体重がなかったんだ。モデルでいるってことはある意味非常に不健康なことなんだ。

Diana: Really? I didn't know that. Dieting can be very dangerous then, can't it?

本当なの？それは知らなかったわ。それじゃあ、ダイエットは非常に危険ってことなの？

John: You're right in a sense, but sometimes it's necessary to go on a diet to improve your health. A **well-balanced diet** with **proper exercise** is the most important part of staying healthy.

ある意味正しい。でも、健康を改善するためにダイエットすることが時には必要になるんだ。適度な運動とバランスのとれた食事が健康を保つ上で最も重要な部分なんだ。

Diana: I will **keep your advice in mind the next time**

次にダイエットする時に

I go on a diet.　　　　　　　　　　　　　　はあなたのアドバイスを心に留めておくわ。

Words & Phrases

- get skinnier　やせる
- pay too much attention to 〜　〜に多くの注意を払いすぎる
- pop stars and models　人気歌手やモデル
- thin　細い、やせた
- get teased　からかわれる
- lose weight　体重を減らす
- dieting　ダイエット
- dietary supplement　栄養補助食品
- go on a diet　ダイエットをする
- purpose　目的
- immediately　すぐに、早急に
- die of 〜　〜が原因で死ぬ
- centimeter　センチメートル
- weigh　〜の体重がある
- well-balanced diet　バランスのとれた食事
- proper exercise　適度な運動
- keep one's advice in mind　アドバイスを心に留める
- the next time 〜　この次〜する時に

Tips　よく使われる表現―ためらい②―

- you're right in a sense, but ～
  （あなたはある意味正しい、しかし～）
- what you've just said is right, but ～
  （あなたが今言ったことは正しい、しかし～）
- you're right on that point, but ～
  （あなたはその点では正しい、しかし～）

◆その他の表現

- moreover
  （さらに、その上に）
- that's why
  （そんなわけで、～である）
- So you support the idea of dieting?
  （ダイエットするという考えを支持するのかい。）
- Yes, I support dieting.
  （ダイエットを支持する。）

◆すぐに使える表現　Possible Opinions

- Strict dieting damages your health.
  （厳しいダイエットは、健康を害する。）
- Childhood obesity leads to serious diseases later in life.
  （子供の肥満は、後の人生で深刻な病気につながる。）
- Parents should play a key role in health education.
  （両親は、健康教育において重要な役割を果たすべきである。）
- Eating less to lose weight can lead to poor nutrition.
  （減量するために食事の量を減らすことは、栄養不足につながる。）
- Modifying eating habits is more important than dieting.
  （食習慣を変えることはダイエット以上に大切である。）

ケース 17　サマータイムの是非

Track 17　Daylight-saving time: for or against?

電力不足対策や環境保護のためにサマータイムの導入が叫ばれている。サマータイムの導入は必要なのだろうか。

ダイアローグ
Dialogue

TV anchor: Every summer, there is the same discussion on whether or not Japan should **adopt daylight-saving time**. It has **currently** been adopted by about 80 countries in the **Northern Hemisphere**. The main **aim** of adopting daylight-saving time is to **reduce** the use of energy on lighting and **air-conditioning** in the morning and evening. There are both pros and cons to adopting this system.

毎年夏になると、日本がサマータイムを導入すべきかどうかという同じ議論が起きます。サマータイムは北半球の約80の国々で採用されています。サマータイムを採用する主な目的は、朝晩の電気やエアコンのエネルギー消費量を減らすことです。このシステムの導入については、賛否両論があります。

89

John: This system has another **advantage**. An early start means an early finish. Therefore, people will be able to go home while it's still light out. I hope many people will take this time to play sports or spend time with their families.

このシステムにはもう一つ利点があるんだ。早く始めれば早く終わるってことさ。だから、人々は外がまだ明るい間に、帰宅できるようになるんだ。たくさんの人が、スポーツをしたり、家族と一緒に過ごしたりするためにこの時間を利用してほしいんだ。

Diana: So, you think this is not only an **eco-friendly** system but also a **family-friendly** one?

じゃあ、これが環境にやさしいだけでなく家族にやさしいシステムだと思っているのね。

John: That's right. This is a really good idea.

そのとおりさ。これは本当に良い考えだよ。

Diana: It seems to be a very **sophisticated** system. But I have a simple question about your idea. Do you think people will actually go home earlier?

非常に賢明なシステムに思えるわね。でも私にはあなたの考えについて素朴な疑問があるわ。あなたは人々が早く帰宅できると思うの？

John: What do you mean?

どういう意味？

Diana: The Japanese are **notorious workaholics**. If they **go to their offices** one hour earlier and work **regular office hours**, they will **end up** work**ing** an extra hour.

日本人は、悪名高い仕事中毒でしょう。もし1時間早く出社して通常の勤務時間働いたら、1時間余分に働いたことになるわ。

John: I understand your concern. However, if we don't **take action against global warming** now, we'll **regret** not having done anything. Moreover, the Japanese government **encourages** us **to install solar power generation systems** in our homes. Why, then,

君が心配する気持ちはわかるよ。しかし、もし私たちが今地球温暖化に対して行動を起こさなければ、何もしなかったことに対して後悔することになるよね。さらに、日本の政府は家庭に太陽光発電システムを設置することを奨励しているよ。それなのに、政府がサマータイムを導入することに

ケース17　サマータイムの是非

　　　　　is the government **unwilling to** adopt daylight-saving time? ｜ 気が進まない理由があるんだろうか。

Diana:　You make a good point. ｜ あなたは説得力がありますね。

Words & Phrases

- adopt　〜を導入する
- daylight-saving time　サマータイム
- currently　現在は、今や
- Northern Hemisphere　北半球
- aim　目的、目標
- reduce　〜を減らす
- air-conditioning　冷房、空調
- advantage　強み、有益な点
- eco-friendly　環境にやさしい
- family-friendly　家庭にやさしい
- sophisticated　洗練された
- notorious　悪名高い
- workaholic　仕事中毒
- go to the office　会社に行く
- regular office hours　通常の勤務時間
- end up 〜 ing　結局〜になる
- take action against 〜　〜に対して行動をとる
- global warming　地球温暖化
- regret　〜を後悔する
- encourage … to 〜　…に〜するよう勧める、励ます
- install solar power generation systems　太陽光発電システムを設置する
- be unwilling to 〜　〜することに気が進まない、〜することを嫌がる

Tips よく使われる表現―質問―

☐ I have a simple question about your idea.
　（あなたの考えについて素朴な質問がある。）
☐ I have a question concerning your opinion.
　（あなたの意見について質問がある。）
☐ May I ask a question regarding your idea?
　（あなたの考えについて質問しても良いですか。）
☐ I'd like to ask a question about your opinion.
　（あなたの意見について質問したい。）

◆その他の表現

☐ there are pros and cons to ～
　（～についての賛否両論がある）
☐ therefore
　（そのために）
☐ What do you mean?
　（どういう意味なの？）
☐ I understand your concern.
　（心配する気持ちはわかる。）
☐ however
　（しかし）
☐ moreover
　（さらに）
☐ You make a good point.
　（説得力があるね。）

ケース17　サマータイムの是非

◆すぐに使える表現　Possible Opinions

- Introducing daylight-saving time will reduce crime and traffic accidents because people can go home and go shopping during the day time.
（サマータイムを導入すると、人々がまだ明るい間に帰宅したり、買い物をしたりするので、犯罪や交通事故が減ることになる。）

- Daylight-saving time will generate some billions of dollars worth of economic gains in the leisure and tourism industries.
（サマータイムは、レジャー産業や旅行業界において、何十億ドル相当もの経済効果を出すだろう。）

- Some people may suffer from a significant sleep disorder caused by daylight-saving time.
（サマータイムによる深刻な睡眠障害を患う人々がいるかもしれない。）

- It's troublesome to adjust all the clocks.
（すべての時計を合わせるのは厄介である。）

- Daylight-saving time is a chance for us to change our lifestyles and help combat global warming.
（サマータイムは、我々のライフスタイルを変え、地球温暖化を防ぐひとつのチャンスである。）

- Daylight-saving time aims to make better use of the extended daylight hours in summer.
（サマータイムは、夏の長い日照時間を効果的に活用することを目的とする。）

ケース 18 生徒のアルバイトの是非

Track 18　Students working part-time: for or against?

社会勉強と称して高校生がアルバイトをする。高校生のアルバイトは必要なのだろうか。

ダイアローグ
Dialogue

TV Anchor: **Quite a large number of** young people **borrow** money from **quick-loan outlets** and soon **face financial troubles**. This is partly because they never learned how to earn money or of money's importance during their high school years. Wouldn't it be a good idea for students to **work part-time** while still in high school? That way, students will **realize** the true meaning of work. There are, however,

かなりの人数の若者が、消費者金融からお金を借りて、すぐに金銭トラブルに陥ります。これは一部には、彼らが高校生の時に、お金の稼ぎ方やお金の重要性を学んでいないからです。彼らが、高校在学中にアルバイトをするのは、良い考えではないでしょうか。そうすれば、生徒は、働くことの本当の意義に気づくでしょう。しかし、高校生にアルバイトをさせることには、いまだに賛否両論があります。

still pros and cons to letting high school students work part-time.

John: Are you for or against letting high school students work part-time?

高校生にアルバイトさせることには賛成それとも反対かい？

Diana: I **definitely** think students should be allowed to work part-time. I want to tell you about some of the lessons I've learned through my experiences.

私は、絶対に高校生のアルバイトが許可されるべきだと思うわ。私が経験を通して学んだ教訓をいくつか話したいと思うわ。

John: I'd love to hear them. What exactly are they?

ぜひ聞かせて。それはいったいどんなものなの？

Diana: Well, let me see. I met many people and **made friends with** them. Also, I learned how to communicate with others and improved my **social skills**. I learned so many things. I can't possibly describe them all.

そうね、ええっと。私はたくさんの人々に会って、仲良くなったわ。さらに、他の人とのコミュニケーションのとり方を学びました。そして社交術も向上したわ。私は非常にたくさんのことを学んだわ。おそらくすべて言い尽くせないわ。

John: If what you've said are the main goals of allowing high school students to work part-time, I oppose the idea. Students can learn those skills in high school, especially by joining **extracurricular** activities.

もし君の言うことが高校生にアルバイトを許可する主な目的なら、僕はその考えに反対だね。生徒は高校でもそれらの技術は学ぶことができるよ。特に課外活動に参加することによってね。

Diana: I disagree. How about earning extra money? I couldn't truly appreciate the **value** of a **hard earned dollar** until I earned it myself. I needed to earn money to help my parents

私は反対だわ。臨時収入を稼ぐことはどうなの。自分で稼いではじめて、苦労して稼いだお金の価値に気づくのよ。大学の費用を負担してくれる両親を助けるためにもお金

with the **financial burden** of college. | を稼ぐ必要があったの。

John: You're right in a sense, but if students really need money for college, I **recommend** they **apply for scholarships**. Scholarships are more academically **meaningful** and **profitable** than working part-time. And, to become qualified for scholarships, they have to study hard, so their grades will **improve** as well. | ある意味君は正しいけど、もし生徒が本当に大学へのお金が必要なら、奨学金に応募することを勧めるよ。奨学金は、より学問的に意味があるしアルバイトで働くよりも利益になるよ。それに、奨学金の資格要件を満たすには、生徒は一生懸命勉強しなければならないし、生徒の成績も向上するよ。

Diana: Of course, scholarships help **pay tuition**, but the fact is that not all students **are qualified for** such scholarships. | もちろん、奨学金は学費を払うのに役に立つわ。でも、実際にはすべての生徒が奨学金の資格要件を満たす訳じゃないでしょう。

Words & Phrases

- quite a large number of ～　かなり多くの～
- borrow　～を借りる
- quick-loan outlet　消費者金融
- face financial troubles　金銭トラブルに直面する
- work part-time　アルバイトをする
- realize　～に気がつく、悟る
- definitely　確かに、間違いなく
- make friends with ～　～と親しくなる
- social skill　社交術
- extracurricular　カリキュラム外の
- value　価値
- hard earned dollar　苦労して稼いだお金
- financial burden　経済的負担
- recommend　～を勧める
- apply for scholarship　奨学金に応募する
- meaningful　意味のある
- profitable　利益になる、役に立つ
- improve　～を改善する
- pay tuition　授業料を払う
- be qualified for ～　～する資格がある

ケース18 生徒のアルバイトの是非

Tips よく使われる表現—確認①—

- What exactly are they?
  (それらは一体何なのですか。)
- What exactly do you mean?
  (一体何が言いたいのですか。)
- What exactly are you driving at?
  (一体何が言いたいのですか。)
- What exactly are you getting at?
  (一体何が言いたいのですか。)

◆その他の表現

- this is partly because ～
  (これは一部には～だからです)
- there are pros and cons to ～
  (～に関して賛否両論があります)
- are you for or against ～
  (～に賛成ですか反対ですか)
- I oppose the idea.
  (私はその考えには反対である。)
- I disagree.
  (私は賛成しない。)
- How about earning extra money?
  (臨時収入を稼ぐことについては、どう思うの？)
- you're right in a sense, but ～
  (ある意味、君は正しいが、～)
- the fact is that ～
  (実は、～である)

◆ すぐに使える表現　Possible Opinions

- It's necessary to know the importance of saving and setting financial goals by working part-time.
  （アルバイトをすることによって、倹約や貯蓄目標を設定する重要性を知ることは必要である。）
- You spend 8 hours a day at school, one hour working on your homework, and a few more hours working part-time. Is it possible?
  （毎日学校で8時間過ごし、宿題に1時間かけ、さらにアルバイトに数時間過ごす。それが可能なの？）
- What's the purpose of earning money through a part-time job?
  （アルバイトでお金を稼ぐ目的は何なの？）
- It's a good chance to learn about the business world.
  （ビジネス社会について学ぶ良い機会である。）
- You'll have no time for homework.
  （宿題するための時間がない。）

ケース 19 ハイテクトイレの是非
Track 19　High-tech toilets: for or against?

日本のトイレは、世界的に見ても類を見ないほど進化している。ハイテクトイレは必要なのだろうか。

ダイアローグ / Dialogue

TV anchor: A Japanese **gadget** that had once surprised and **confused** many foreign visitors was the **high-tech toilet**. Now, it **attracts** the **curiosity** of many visitors from abroad. They **get addicted to** using one during their stay in their hotel, buy a high-tech toilet and bring it back home. Having such toilets in one's house is a **status symbol** in some countries.

多くの外国からの訪問者を驚かせ、当惑させていた日本の装置は、ハイテクトイレです。今、ハイテクトイレは海外からの多くの訪問者の好奇心をかき立てています。ホテル滞在中にハイテクトイレにやみつきになっていて、ハイテクトイレを買い、自国へ持ち帰っています。自分の家で、そのようなトイレがあることが、いくつかの国々ではステータスシンボルとなっています。

John:	What do you think of this news?	このニュースについてどう思う？
Diana:	Such toilets are convenient and **comfortable** with a **heated seat**, a water jet bidet and a **blow dryer**. I like high-tech toilets, too.	ハイテクトイレは、保温便座、ウォータージェットビデや温風乾燥機がついていて、便利で快適だよ。私もハイテクトイレは好きだわ。
John:	That's exactly what I think, but that's also the problem.	僕も同感だよ、でもそれも問題なんだ。
Diana:	Really? What's wrong, then?	それのどこが悪いの？
John:	I'm talking about **environmental issues**. Take water, for instance. A high-tech toilet is a water **guzzler, accounting for** about 30 percent of average **household water consumption**. Besides, high-tech toilets **require** more electricity than **conventional toilets**.	僕は、環境問題について話しているんだ。水を例にとると、ハイテクトイレは、大量に水を消費するんだ。平均的な家庭の水使用量の30％を占めているんだ。その上、ハイテクトイレは、従来の便器と比べ、より多くの電気を消費するんだ。
Diana:	I find it difficult to support your opinion. Such toilets are very comfortable and **allow me to** relax, so I don't mind spending a little extra money.	私には、あなたの意見を支持するのは難しいと思うわ。ハイテクトイレは、とても快適で、リラックスさせてくれるんですもの。だから、多少お金がかかっても気にしないわ。
John:	What I want to say here is that high-tech toilets are **user-friendly**, but they are not **environmentally friendly**. They **consume** a lot of water while a lot of people in the world **face water shortages**. We mustn't be too **selfish** because we are not the only people on	僕がここで言いたいことは、ハイテクトイレは使い勝手が良いけど、環境にはやさしくないということだよ。世界中でたくさんの人々が水不足に直面しているのに、ハイテクトイレは、かなり大量の水を消費しているんだ。僕たちだけが地球上に住んでいるわけじゃないので自分たちだけのこ

the planet.

Diana: I like what you've just said. What you're trying to say is more environmentally friendly toilets should be **developed**, right?

とを考えるべきではないんだ。

私は、あなたが今言ったことが気に入ったわ。あなたが言いたいことは、もっと環境にやさしいトイレが開発されるべきだということよね？

John: Yes, that's what I'm saying.

そう、それが僕の言いたいことだよ。

Words & Phrases

- gadget　装置
- confused　困惑した、混乱した
- high-tech toilet　ハイテクトイレ、最新式トイレ
- attract　〜を引きつける
- curiosity　好奇心
- get addicted to 〜　〜に病みつきになる
- status symbol　地位の象徴
- comfortable　くつろいだ
- heated seat　保温便座
- blow dryer　温風乾燥機
- environmental issue　環境問題
- guzzler　ガソリンを大量消費する車、大酒飲み
- account for 〜　〜の割合を占める
- household water consumption　家庭の水使用量
- require　〜を必要とする
- conventional toilet　従来の便器
- allow 〜 to …　〜が…するのを許す
- user-friendly　使い勝手が良い
- environmentally friendly　環境にやさしい
- consume　〜を消費する
- face water shortage　水不足に直面する
- selfish　自分勝手な
- develop　〜を開発する

Tips　よく使われる表現―確認②―

☐ What you're trying to say is ～, right?
　（あなたが言いたいことは～だよね？）
☐ What you want to say is ～, right?
　（あなたが言っていることは～だよね？）
☐ What you mean is ～, right?
　（あなたが言いたいことは～だよね？）

◆その他の表現

☐ What do you think of this news?
　（このニュースをどう思うの？）
☐ That's exactly what I think, but that's the problem.
　（全く同感ですが、それが問題である。）
☐ Take water, for instance.
　（水を例にとってみよう。）
☐ besides
　（その上、さらに）
☐ I find it difficult to support your opinion.
　（あなたの意見を支持するのは難しいと思う。）
☐ What I want to say here is ～.
　（ここで私が言いたいことは～である。）
☐ I like what you've just said.
　（あなたが今言ったことが気に入った。）
☐ Yes, that's what I'm saying.
　（そう、それが私の言いたいことである。）

ケース19　ハイテクトイレの是非

◆ **すぐに使える表現**　Possible Opinions

☐ As consumers, we need to buy toilet seats that consume less energy.
（消費者として、私たちはエネルギーをあまり消費しないトイレ便座を買う必要がある。）

☐ Are high-tech toilets really indispensable for humans?
（ハイテクトイレは人間にとって本当に必要不可欠なのだろうか？）

☐ Which is more important, user-friendly or environmentally friendly products? We have to think which is better for the earth.
（使い勝手がよい製品と環境にやさしい製品のどちらがより重要だろうか。私たちはどちらが地球にとって良いかを考えなくてはならない。）

☐ Technology has definitely made our lives convenient. So without high-tech toilets, for example, we feel inconvenienced.
（科学技術のおかげで、間違いなく私たちの生活は便利になった。だから、例えばハイテクトイレがないと、私たちは不便を感じる。）

ケース 20 美人コンテストの是非

Track 20

Beauty pageants: for or against?

⁉ 女性の魅力を競う美人コンテストについては、賛否両論ある。美人コンテストは必要なのだろうか。

ダイアローグ
Dialogue

TV anchor: A "**man-made**" beauty **pageant** was held in China. **Contestants** could only **qualify for** this pageant if they had **undergone cosmetic surgery**. Thanks to cosmetic surgery, a 62-year-old woman was chosen as one of 19 **finalists** in the pageant.

整形美人コンテストが中国で開催されました。出場者は、美容整形手術を受けている場合のみ、この美人コンテストに出場する資格を得ることができます。美容整形手術のおかげで、62歳の女性が美人コンテストの19人の決勝戦出場者の1人として選抜されました。

John: Are you interested in beauty pageants?

美人コンテストに興味ある？

Diana: Yes, I am. As a woman, I enjoy seeing

ええあるわ。女性として美しいスタイルや顔を見

beautiful figures and faces. I admire their efforts to become more beautiful.

John: So, do you support the pageants? I think beauty pageants just **promote** the **plastic surgery** business and cosmetics sales. I hear many women try to change themselves to fit the **ideal image** of beauty. **That sounds strange to me.**

Diana: Really? Why do you think so? Could you elaborate on that, please?

John: Well, due to beauty pageants, many women try dieting, **suffer from eating disorders** and undergo plastic surgery. In my opinion, truly beautiful women should not only have outer beauty, but also **inner beauty**, **intelligence** and **modesty**.

Diana: That kind of makes sense. But the reality is that millions of dollars are spent on cosmetics. Moreover, thousands of dollars are spent on plastic surgery and much more money is spent on dieting.

John: That much?

Diana: Yeah. That's ordinary women.

Words & Phrases

- man-made 人工の、人間が作り出した
- pageant ショー
- contestant 出場者
- qualify for ~ ~の参加資格を得る
- undergo cosmetic surgery 美容整形手術を受ける
- finalist 決勝戦出場者
- beautiful figure 美しいプロポーション、美しい姿
- promote ~を宣伝する
- plastic surgery 美容整形手術
- ideal image 理想のイメージ
- That sounds strange to me. 変に聞こえるわ。
- suffer from eating disorder 摂食障害で苦しむ
- inner beauty 内面の美しさ
- intelligence 知性
- modesty つつましさ、控えめ

Tips よく使われる表現 ―確認③―

- Could you elaborate on what you said, please?
  (あなたが言ったことについて詳しく説明していただけますか。)
- Could you give me more information about it?
  (それについてもっと情報をいただけませんか。)
- Can you be more specific about your proposal, please?
  (あなたの提案についてもっと具体的に話していただけますか。)
- Please explain further concerning your idea.
  (あなたの考えについてもっと詳しく説明してください。)

◆その他の表現

- thanks to ~
  (~のおかげで、結果)
- Do you support the pageants?
  (そのコンテストを支持するのですか。)
- due to ~
  (~が原因で)

☐ in one's opinion
　(〜の意見では)
☐ That kind of makes sense.
　(それは一理あるね。)
☐ the reality is that 〜
　(実は〜である)
☐ moreover
　(さらに)

◆すぐに使える表現　Possible Opinions

☐ Each country should maintain its own ideal of beauty, rather than conforming to western standards.
　(それぞれの国は、西洋の規準に合わせるよりはむしろ自国の理想とする美を保持すべきである。)
☐ Beauty pageants give women a chance to get noticed by the world.
　(美人コンテストは女性に世界で認められるチャンスを与える。)
☐ Beauty pageants objectify women.
　(美人コンテストは女性をものとして見なす。)
☐ I don't think it's proper to undergo cosmetic surgery to take part in beauty pageants.
　(美人コンテストに出場するために美容整形外科手術を受けるのは適切だとは思わない。)

ケース21 救急車の有料化の是非
Track 21 Charging ambulance fees: for or against?

本当に救急車の出動が必要な人もいるが、緊急性の低い場合にも救急車出動を要請する常識のない人もいる。救急車有料化は必要なのだろうか。

ダイアローグ
Dialogue

TV anchor: The number of **ambulance requests**, especially **those for non-emergency cases**, has **steadily increased** every year. For example, people who are **suffering from** minor health problems such as a **finger-cut** or a **headache** have begun to call 119. Due to this, non-emergency calls are **interfering with** the jobs of **ambulance attendants**.

特に緊急でないケースに対して救急車を要請する数が、毎年確実に増加しています。例えば、指の切り傷や頭痛などのちょっとした体調不良の人が119番に電話をかけ始めました。このため、緊急でない電話が原因で、救急隊員の仕事が妨害されています。

ケース21　救急車の有料化の是非

Diana: Did you hear that? I am surprised to find out that a lot of 119 calls are made for non-emergency cases.

これ聞きました？たくさんの119番への電話が緊急でないケースに対してかけられているって知って驚きよね。

John: Me, too. I thought patients who made 119 calls were those who really **needed immediate attention**. Are there any ways to **reduce** the number of non-emergency calls?

僕も驚いたよ。僕は119番に電話する患者は本当に早急の手当てを必要とする人々だけだと思ってたよ。緊急以外の電話を減らす方法はあるのかな。

Diana: I've got an idea. Fire departments should fine those who make calls for non-emergencies.

考えがあるわ。消防署は緊急でない電話をした人には罰金を科すべきだわ。

John: I don't agree with you. It's difficult for us to judge how serious a situation is. Besides, who knows if one needs **emergency medical assistance** or not without **consulting a medical professional**?

僕は賛成できないよ。どれだけ深刻な状況か判断するのは僕たちには難しいよ。それに、医療専門家に相談しないで、救急隊を必要としているかどうかがわかる人なんているの？

Diana: Yeah, that's the problem. How about adopting a **basic charge system**?

そうね。それは問題よね。基本料金制を導入するのはどうかしら。

John: What do you have in mind?

どういうこと？

Diana: Well, whether patients are **mildly** or seriously ill, all those taken in an ambulance will have to pay **a certain amount of** money—**say about** $50. That way, patients will understand ambulances are not free taxis.

ええ。患者が軽傷であれ、重傷であれ、救急車で搬送された人はすべて、一定額のお金、例えば50ドルを払わなくてはならないようにするのよ。そうすれば、患者は、救急車が無料タクシーではないと理解するわ。

109

John: I like your idea. 君の考えが気に入ったよ。

Words & Phrases

- ambulance request　救急車の要請
- those who 〜　〜する人々
- non-emergency case　緊急でないケース
- steadily　着実に
- increase　増える
- suffer from 〜　〜を受ける、〜を被る
- finger-cut　指の切り傷
- headache　頭痛
- 119　警察署、消防署、救急車を呼び出すための電話番号
- interfere with 〜　〜を妨げる
- ambulance attendant　救急隊員
- need immediate attention　すぐ対応する必要がある
- reduce　〜を減らす
- emergency medical assistance　救急隊
- consult a medical professional　医療専門家に相談する
- basic charge system　基本料金制
- mildly　少し
- a certain amount of 〜　ある程度の〜、一定の〜
- say about $50　例えば、約50ドル

Tips よく使われる表現―提案①―

- how about 〜？
  (〜はどうですか)
- why don't we 〜？
  (〜しませんか)
- what do you say to 〜 ing?
  (〜はどうですか)
- have you thought about 〜？
  (〜は考えたことがありますか)
- Do you have any ideas?
  (何か考えがありますか。)

◆その他の表現

- due to 〜
  (〜のせいで、〜が原因で)
- are there any ways to 〜？
  (〜する何か方法はある？)
- I've got an idea.
  (私に考えがある。)
- I don't agree with you.
  (あなたには同意しない。)
- besides
  (さらに)
- What do you have in mind?
  (何を考えているの？)

◆すぐに使える表現　Possible Opinions

- If an ambulance is carrying a non-urgent patient, it's difficult for the fire department to dispatch that ambulance to someone with a serious illness.
（救急車が急を要しない患者を運んでいる際に、消防署が、重病患者のために救急車を出動させることは難しい。）

- Ambulance attendants cannot do their duties because of unnecessary calls.
（不必要な電話のせいで救急隊員は自分の職務を果たせない。）

- Some people make false 119 calls. Such people should be severely penalized.
（119番へのいたずら電話をする人がいる。そのような人々には厳しくペナルティーを科すべきである。）

- Charging fees might prevent the seriously ill from calling 119.
（料金を科すことで重症患者が119番への通報をしなくなるかもしれない。）

ケース 22　小学校での英語教育の是非

Track 22　English education in primary school: for or against?

小学校での英語教育に対する期待は大きいが、さまざまな問題がある。小学校における英語教育の充実は図れるだろうか。

Dialogue / ダイアローグ

TV anchor: In 2011, English became **compulsory** in **primary school** in Japan. It's taught by homeroom teachers once a week at the 5th and 6th grade levels. There are a number of pros and cons concerning this issue.

2011年、日本では、英語が小学校で必修化されました。英語は、5年生と6年生で週に1回学級担任が教えます。この問題に関しては、たくさん賛否両論があります。

John: Do you agree with the idea of teaching English in primary school?

小学校で英語を教える考えには賛成かい？

Diana: Yeah, I agree with it. Young learners are said to **develop correct pronunciation of English** quickly. Besides, they **are not nervous about** trying to speak English. What do you think?

ええ、賛成よ。子供たちは、英語の正しい発音を身につけるのが早いと言われているわ。しかも、彼らは、英語を話そうとすることに緊張しないしね。あなたはどう思うの？

John: Basically I agree. But there are some problems.

基本的には賛成だね。しかしいくつか問題があるんだ。

Diana: Really? What are they?

本当に？ どんな問題なの？

John: As the news said, homeroom teachers **are in charge of** lessons. Actually, they are not trained to teach English to young learners. Most of the homeroom teachers hadn't **expected** to teach English when they became teachers.

ニュースでもあったように、学級担任が授業を担当するんだ。実は、彼らは、子供たちに英語を教えるためのトレーニングを受けていないんだ。学級担任のほとんどが、教師になった時、英語を教えることを期待されていなかったんだ。

Diana: I know there might be a lot to say about homeroom teachers, but in today's **global society**, English is a **must**. Besides, regarding language learning, **it is often said that the earlier, the better**.

学級担任について言いたいことがたくさんあるかもしれないのはわかるわ。でも、今日のグローバル社会では、英語は必須条件なの。それに、言語習得に関しては、早ければ早いほど良いって言うでしょう。

John: I fully agree with you there. However, I'm afraid we might be facing an **English divide** between rich and poor cities. I've heard some rich cities have started to **hire** English teachers and **assistant language teachers on**

僕はその点では、大賛成さ。しかし、裕福な市と貧しい市との間で、イングリッシュディバイド（英語格差）に直面するかもしれないね。裕福な市は、独自に英語の教師や外国語指導助手を雇い始めたそうだよ。一方、

their own. **Meanwhile**, poorer cities **are unable to** even provide the chance to learn teaching **methods** to homeroom teachers.

貧しい市は、学級担任に対して教授法を学ぶ機会を提供することさえできないんだ。

Diana: I understand your point. But I strongly believe it's necessary for young learners to **become familiar with** English **regardless of** how it's taught.

あなたの言いたいことはわかるわ。でも、英語の教え方にかかわらず、若い学習者が英語に慣れ親しむことは必要だと強く信じているわ。

Words & Phrases

- compulsory 強制された、必修の
- primary school 小学校
- develop correct pronunciation of English 英語の正しい発音を身につける
- be nervous about ~ ~に神経質である
- be in charge of ~ ~を担当している
- expect ~を予期する
- global society グローバル社会
- must 必需品、必要不可欠
- it is often said that the earlier, the better 「早ければ早い程よい。」とよく言われる
- English divide イングリッシュディバイド（英語格差）
- hire ~を雇う
- assistant language teacher 外国語指導助手
- on one's own 独自で
- meanwhile その一方で
- be unable to ~ ~することができない
- method 方法
- become familiar with ~ ~に慣れ親しむ
- regardless of ~ ~にかかわらず

Tips よく使われる表現―理解―

- ☐ I understand your point.
  (あなたの言いたいことは理解している。)
- ☐ I get your meaning.
  (あなたが言っていることはわかる。)
- ☐ I understand exactly what you're talking about.
  (あなたが言っていることは正確にわかる。)
- ☐ I understand what you mean.
  (あなたが言っていることはわかる。)
- ☐ I catch your drift.
  (あなたの言っていることはわかる。)

◆ その他の表現

- ☐ There are a number of pros and cons concerning this issue.
  (この問題に関してたくさんの賛否両論がある。)
- ☐ do you agree with the idea of ～ ?
  (～の考えに賛成ですか)
- ☐ Yeah, I agree with it.
  (はい、それに賛成です。)
- ☐ What do you think?
  (どう思うの？)
- ☐ Basically I agree. But there are some problems.
  (基本的に賛成です。しかしいくつか問題がある。)
- ☐ I fully agree with you there.
  (私は全面的に賛成です。)
- ☐ however
  (しかし)

ケース22　小学校での英語教育の是非

◆すぐに使える表現　Possible Opinions

- [ ] Most parents agree to introducing English in primary school.
（ほとんどの親は、小学校で英語が導入されることに賛成している。）
- [ ] There are other more important subjects students should study in primary school.
（小学校には、児童が学習すべきより重要な教科が他にある。）
- [ ] Children are not afraid of speaking English in front of others.
（子供たちは、他人の前で英語を話すことを怖れない。）
- [ ] Children have a big advantage in learning correct English pronunciation.
（子供たちは、正しい英語の発音を身につける点で非常に有利である。）
- [ ] There are not enough quality English teachers at the primary school level.
（小学校段階では、よい英語の教員が十分にいない。）

ケース 23　動物実験の是非
Track 23　Animal testing: for or against?

ヨーロッパでは化粧品の動物実験の完全禁止を実現している国が多い。現在行われている動物実験は必要なのだろうか。

ダイアローグ
Dialogue

TV anchor: Every year about 300 million animals around the world are used as **subjects** in **experiments**. They are used in **safety tests** for food, **chemicals** and drugs. Scientists are trying to develop **alternative** testing methods, but in some drug and cosmetic testing, it's impossible to **replace** animals.

毎年、世界中で3億匹もの動物が実験台として使われています。それらは、食物、化学物質や薬品の安全性検査に使われます。科学者は、別の実験方法を開発しようとしていますが、薬品や化粧品の検査の中には、動物実験に取って代わる方法を開発することは不可能なものがあります。

John: What do you think about this problem? I

この問題についてはどう

ケース23　動物実験の是非

	mean, are you for animal testing?	思う？つまり、君は動物実験に賛成なの？
Diana:	I'm opposed to it. Animals' rights should be **protected**.	私は反対よ。動物の権利は保護されるべきよ。
John:	You're partially right, but animal testing is necessary for the development of **vaccines** and **cures** for human **illnesses**. But, I didn't know the number of animals tested on was so large.	君は部分的には正しい、でも、動物実験は、病気のワクチンや治療薬の開発に必要なんだ。でも、実験台にされた動物の数がそれ程多いとは知らなかったな。
Diana:	You've got a point there. I don't think it's possible to **ban** all animal testing. Nevertheless, it's possible for us to **decrease** the number of animals killed. I'm sure animals feel and **suffer pain** the same way humans do. Would you allow your pet to be a test subject?	その点では一理あるわね。私も、すべての動物実験を禁止することが可能だと思わないわ。そうは言っても動物実験に殺される数を減らすことは可能でしょう。動物だって人間が感じるのと同様に痛みを感じるはずよ。自分のペットが実験台になることを許せる？
John:	Of course not. **Stick to the point.**	もちろん許さないよ。論点をそらさないでくれよ。
Diana:	I think it's important to do as much as we can to **reduce** animal testing. In fact, just **the other day** I **signed a petition** against animal testing. Also, I try not to buy **animal-tested cosmetics**. I look for **labels** that say, "This product is not tested on animals."	動物実験を減らすために、私たちができるだけ多くのことをすることは大切だと思うわ。実は、先日動物実験に反対する陳情書に署名したわ。それに、動物実験が行われている化粧品は買わないようにしているわ。「この製品は動物実験をしていません」というラベルを探すのよ。
John:	I'm glad to hear that. In that way, we can	それを聞いて嬉しいよ。

help decrease the number of animals used in experiments.

そんな風に、私たちは実験で使われる動物の数を減らすことに協力できるね。

Diana: Plus, companies and **researchers** should **reconsider** the necessity of animal testing because tons of animals die in experiments yearly.

それに企業や研究者が動物実験の必要性を再考すべきだわ。毎年、莫大な数の動物が実験で死んでいるのだから。

Words & Phrases

- subject （実験の）被験者、対象
- experiment 実験
- safety test 安全性検査
- chemical 化学物質
- alternative 代替の
- replace ～を交換する
- protect ～を守る
- vaccine ワクチン
- cure 治療、治療薬（法）
- illness 病気
- ban ～を禁じる
- decrease ～を減らす
- suffer pain 苦痛を感じる
- Stick to the point. 問題からそれないようにする。
- reduce ～を減らす
- the other day 先日
- sign a petition 陳情書に署名する
- animal-tested cosmetic （製造過程で）動物実験が行われた化粧品
- label ラベル
- researcher 研究者
- reconsider ～を再考する

Tips よく使われる表現 —一定の理解—

- you're partially right, but 〜
  (部分的にあなたは正しい、が〜)
- There is some truth in what you are trying to say.
  (あなたが言おうとしていることに一理ある。)
- He's not completely wrong, you know.
  (彼の言うことすべてが間違っている訳ではない。)
- In one way, you are right.
  (ある意味では、あなたは正しい。)

◆その他の表現

- What do you think about this problem?
  (この問題についてどう思うの？)
- I mean, are you for animal testing?
  (つまり、動物実験に賛成ということなの？)
- I'm opposed to it.
  (私はそれに反対である。)
- You've got a point there.
  (それも一理あるね。)
- nevertheless
  (それにもかかわらず)
- in fact
  (実際に)
- plus
  (さらに)

◆すぐに使える表現　Possible Opinions

☐ We must do tests on animals or humans to develop life-saving drugs.
（生命を救う医薬品を開発するために、動物や人間で検査しなければならない。）

☐ Humans have a choice whether to do animal testing or not.
（人間には、動物実験をするかどうか選択権がある。）

☐ It's up to humans, because animals can't ask for help.
（人間次第である。なぜなら、動物は助けを求めることができないから。）

☐ It's important to develop methods to ease the pain of the animals tested.
（実験で使われる動物の痛みを和らげるための方法を開発することは大切である。）

☐ We should protect animals' rights.
（私たちは動物の権利を守るべきである。）

ケース24 飲酒の是非

Track 24

Drinking alcohol: for or against?

⁉ 適量の飲酒は、ストレスの緩和や食欲増進に効果を発揮するというが、人により適量は異なる。飲酒はどの程度必要なのだろうか。

ダイアローグ
Dialogue

TV anchor: A famous singer was **arrested** when he was found drunk and **naked** in a park. According to the police, he **got intoxicated** at a pub and **fell into a state** where he couldn't **control himself**. At the **press conference**, he said he was **ashamed** and **deeply regretted** his actions.

有名な歌手が、公園で酔って裸になっているところを発見され、逮捕されました。警察によると、彼はパブで泥酔し、自制することができない状態に陥ったとのことです。記者会見では、彼は自分の行動を恥じ、深く後悔しているということでした。

Diana: Did you hear about this?

これ聞いた？

John: Yes, I heard. I'm **astonished** by the news. I really **admire** him **as** a **talented** dancer and singer. He **is** also **famous as** a **serious actor**.

うん、聞いたよ。ニュースには驚いたね。僕は、彼を才能あるダンサー、歌手として尊敬していたのに。彼は正統派俳優としても有名だよ。

Diana: You're right. I think he is admired by people of all ages because he is so **multitalented**. Too bad drinking alcohol **damaged his career quite a bit**.

そうよね。彼は多才だから、あらゆる年齢層から支持されていたと思うわ。残念な飲酒のせいでかなり彼の経歴に傷がついたわね。

John: Yeah. By the way, are you opposed to the drinking of alcohol?

そうだね。ところで、飲酒には反対かい？

Diana: Yes, I am. I don't think drinking is a good thing at all.

そうね。飲酒が良いことだとは全く思わないの。

John: Personally, I don't think there's anything wrong with drinking. It helps **break the ice** between **coworkers** with whom I **have little in common** and myself. Without alcohol, I don't think many of my coworkers could talk to each other. Besides, it's **normal** for everyone to drink at parties. I feel sorry for people who don't drink because they seem very **isolated**.

個人的には、僕には、飲酒の何が悪いのかわからないよ。飲酒は、共通点がほとんどない私と同僚との間の堅苦しさを取り払うのに役に立つんだ。アルコール無しでは、私の同僚の多くがお互いに深く話せないと思う。しかも、パーティーで飲むのは普通だよね。飲めない人は気の毒に思うよ。孤立しているように見えるからね。

Diana: I'm sure they have **good reasons** for not drinking which are **none of your business**. Some people don't drink alcohol because they just don't like it. Plus, you forget that drinking alcohol also causes thousands of **ailments**.

飲まない人には他人にはわからない正当な理由がきっとあるのよ。お酒が好きじゃないので飲まない人もいるわ。しかも、飲酒がいろいろな病気を引き起こすことをあなたは忘れているわ。

For example, it can cause high **blood pressure** or **worsen diabetes**. Moreover, there are social problems like **alcoholism** and **drunk driving**.

例えば、高血圧を引き起こしたり、糖尿病を悪化させたりするのよ。さらにアルコール依存症や飲酒運転という社会問題もあるわ。

John: I know you're right. I should be careful, but drinking does have its **benefits**. I think **it does more good than harm** when people drink **in moderation**.

そうだよね。僕はもっと注意すべきだね。でも、飲酒にもメリットはあるんだ。適度に飲めば害を与える以上に利益をもたらすと思うんだ。

Words & Phrases

- arrest　〜を逮捕する
- naked　裸の
- get intoxicated　酔う
- fall into a state 〜　〜の状態に陥る
- control oneself　自制する
- press conference　記者会見
- ashamed　恥じている
- deeply regret　深く後悔している
- astonish　〜を驚かす
- admire 〜 as …　〜を…として称賛する
- talented　才能のある
- be famous as 〜　〜として有名である
- serious actor　正統派の役者
- multitalented　多才な
- damage one's career　〜のキャリアを傷つける
- quite a bit　かなりたくさんの
- break the ice　緊張をほぐす、口火を切る
- coworker　同僚
- have little in common　共通点がほとんどない
- normal　普通の、通常の
- isolated　孤立した
- good reason　正当な理由、よほどの事情
- (It's) none of one's business.　〜にかかわりのないこと。
- ailment　病気
- blood pressure　血圧
- worsen diabetes　糖尿病を悪化させる
- alcoholism　アルコール依存症
- drunk driving　飲酒運転
- benefit　メリット
- it does more good than harm　害を与える以上に利益をもたらす
- in moderation　適度に

Tips　よく使われる表現―因果関係―

☐ cause
　　（～を引き起こす）
☐ lead to ～
　　（～を引き起こす、結果として～になる）
☐ bring about ～
　　（～を引き起こす、～をもたらす）
☐ generate
　　（～を引き起こす、～を発生させる）

◆その他の表現

☐ according to the police
　　（警察によれば）
☐ Did you hear about this?
　　（これについて聞きましたか。）
☐ By the way, are you opposed to drinking of alcohol?
　　（ところで飲酒運転は反対なの？）
☐ I don't think there's anything wrong with drinking.
　　（飲酒に関して特に悪い事があるとは思えない。）
☐ besides
　　（さらに）
☐ plus
　　（加えて、さらに）
☐ for example
　　（例えば）
☐ moreover
　　（さらに）

ケース24　飲酒の是非

◆すぐに使える表現　Possible Opinions

☐ Drinking can relieve stress.
（飲酒はストレスを和らげてくれる。）

☐ Drinking can enliven conversation and bring people closer.
（飲酒は会話を活気づけ、お互いを親密にする。）

☐ Alcohol relaxes the body and can help to relieve insomnia.
（アルコールは体をリラックスさせ不眠症を和らげる助けとなる。）

☐ People are more likely to commit crimes like assault, rape, and even murder under the influence of alcohol.
（人々は酒に酔うと暴力、強姦、殺人の罪を犯す傾向が強い。）

☐ People suffer from hangovers after drinking too much.
（人々は飲みすぎた後、二日酔いに苦しむ。）

☐ It's fine to enjoy alcohol alone, but one cannot become so drunk that they become a nuisance to those around them.
（一人でアルコールを嗜むのは結構である。しかし周りの人に迷惑になるほど、飲みすぎてはならない。）

ケース 25 独身者のための結婚仲介業者の是非

Track 25 — Matchmaking agencies for single people: for or against?

会員制の結婚情報サービスが一般化している。従来あったお見合いの現代版は必要なのだろうか。

ダイアローグ
Dialogue

TV anchor: **Local governments** plan to **designate certain matchmaking agencies** for single people as **reliable organizations** if they **meet a set of prescribed conditions**. **Unmarried** people are then **motivated** to use the agencies that have been **regarded as** reliable. In doing this, the governments want to increase the number of births by increasing the number of **marriages**.

地方自治体は、一連の所定条件を満たせば、独身者のためのある結婚仲介業を信頼できる機関として指定する計画です。未婚者は、信頼できるとみなされた仲介業者となれば、利用しやすくなります。地方自治体は結婚の数を増やすことで出生者数の増加を見込んでいます。

John: Do you think matchmaking agencies are a good idea?

結婚仲介業者は良い考えだと思う？

Diana: Yes, I'm all for it. These agencies' systems are **improved versions** of traditional **arranged marriages**. Unmarried people first **screen profiles** for their **ideal** partner. Then, they can check the potential partner's **characteristics**, **personal income** and family information to **make a decision**.

そうね。全面的に賛成よ。これらの業者システムは伝統的なお見合いの改良版ね。未婚の人は、理想のパートナーをプロフィールを見てふるいにかけるのね。そうしてパートナー候補の性格、個人所得、家族情報を確認し、決断できるのよ。

John: I don't think a written profile can **give** you a **complete picture of** a person.

僕は、書面の略歴では、個人の全体像が見えるとは思えないね。

Diana: That's why they also have dating parties organized by the agencies. If two people like each other, they can continue dating until they make a final decision.

だから業者が企画するお見合いパーティーもあるのよ。もしお互いが気に入れば、最終決断を下すまでお付き合いを続けられるのよ。

John: What do you think about falling in love? I think it's natural for people to meet and fall in love in daily life. There are many styles of love, such as first love, office love, **long-distance love** and so on. As a typical guy, I'd like to fall in love **by chance**.

恋愛についてはどう思う？人々が日常生活の中で、出会い恋に落ちるのが自然だと思うな。恋愛には多くの形があるよ。例えば一目惚れ、社内恋愛、遠距離恋愛などね。典型的な男性として、僕は運命的に恋に落ちてみたいよ。

Diana: I get what you are saying. But, everybody has a different personality. Some are **awkward** and shy. Some are confident and **persuasive**

あなたの言いたいことはわかるわ。でも、みんな性格が違うのよ。不器用で恥ずかしがり屋の人もいるわ。あなたのように

like you. Some are **romantic** and **passionate** like me. Therefore, it is sometimes hard for some to find partners on their own.

自信に満ちて説得力のある人もいる。私のようにロマンティックで情熱的な人もいる。だから、独力で自分のパートナーを見つけることが難しい場合もあるの。

John:: What are you implying?

何が言いたいの？

Diana: Of course not everybody needs matchmaking agencies. However, I'm sure some need this system to find proper partners.

もちろん、すべての人が結婚仲介業者を必要としている訳ではないわ。でも、適当なパートナーを見つけるためにこのシステムを必要としている人がいるのは確かよ。

Words & Phrases

- Local government　地方自治体
- designate　〜を指名する、〜を指定する
- certain　ある、わずかの
- matchmaking agency　結婚仲介業者
- reliable organization　信頼できる機関
- meet a set of prescribed condition
　一連の所定条件を満たす
- unmarried　未婚者
- motivate　〜する気にさせる
- regard 〜 as …　〜を…とみなす
- marriage　結婚
- improved version　改良型
- arranged marriage　見合い結婚
- screen profile　プロフィールで選抜する、ふるいにかける
- ideal　理想的な
- characteristics　特徴
- personal income　個人所得
- make a decision　決心する
- give complete picture of 〜　〜の全体像を示す
- long-distance love　長距離恋愛
- by chance　偶然に
- awkward　不器用な
- persuasive　説得力がある
- romantic　ロマンチックな
- passionate　情熱的な

ケース25 独身者のための結婚仲介業者の是非

Tips よく使われる表現—理由①—

- [ ] that's why 〜
 (それで〜)
- [ ] for this reason
 (こういう訳で)
- [ ] because of that
 (そのため)
- [ ] it follows from this that 〜
 (このことから判断すると〜ということになる)

◆その他の表現

- [ ] Do you think matchmaking agencies are a good idea?
 (結婚相談所は良い考えだと思う？)
- [ ] I'm all for it.
 (全面的にそれに賛成です。)
- [ ] What do you think about falling in love?
 (恋に落ちることについてどう思うの？)
- [ ] I get what you are saying.
 (あなたが言っていることは、わかった。)
- [ ] therefore
 (それゆえに、そのため)
- [ ] What are you implying?
 (何が言いたいの？)

◆すぐに使える表現　Possible Opinions

- ☐ Agencies need to explain the contract thoroughly to customers before they sign it.
  （仲介業者は顧客が契約書に署名する前に、契約書を完全に説明する必要がある。）
- ☐ Men and women need to learn to express their feelings for each other.
  （男性も女性もお互いの気持ちを表現する方法を身につける必要がある。）
- ☐ People need communication skills to make others feel relaxed or comfortable.
  （お互いをリラックスさせ快適にさせるコミュニケーションスキルを必要とする。）
- ☐ I don't want to depend on matchmaking agencies to find a partner.
  （結婚相手を見つけるのに結婚仲介業者に頼りたくない。）
- ☐ I believe that the man of my destiny lives somewhere in this world. I'd like to meet him on my own.
  （私の運命の人がこの世界のどこかにいると信じている。自力で彼に会ってみたい。）

ケース26 血液型と性格との関係の是非

Track 26　The link between blood type and character: for or against?

⁉️ 血液型と性格との関係で話が盛り上がることがある。血液型と性格との関係はあるのだろうか。

ダイアローグ
Dialogue

TV anchor: **Believe it or not**, it's very **popular** among Japanese people to read books linking **character** to **blood type**. **So far**, a **best-selling series of books** about blood type has sold 5 million copies. A survey says, almost half the people questioned **believe in** the link between blood type and character. Do you believe in it?

信じられないかもしれませんが、日本人の間では、性格と血液型を結びつける本を読むのが大変流行っています。今まで、血液型に関するベストセラーのシリーズ本は、500万部売れました。ある調査によると、回答者のほぼ半分が血液型と性格との関係を信じています。皆さんは信じますか。

Diana: Why is it so popular to **judge** ones' character

どうして、人の性格を血

	by blood type? Actually, I was a bit surprised when asked my blood type **for the first time**.	液型で判断することが流行っているのかしら？実際、初めて血液型を尋ねられた時には少し驚いたわ。
John:	Did you think the person who asked was a **vampire** or something?	尋ねた人が吸血鬼か何かと思ったの？
Diana:	No…, but a lot of people visiting Japan have **similar**, **confusing** experiences. Do you believe in a link between blood type and character?	いいえ。でも、日本を訪れるたくさんの人々が似たような、戸惑った経験をしているの。あなたは血液型と性格の関係を信じているの？
John:	Not at all. I'm a very **realistic** person. On second thought, it's obvious that every characteristic is **determined** by **DNA** and one's **surrounding environment**.	全く信じていないよ。僕は現実的な人間だから。よく考えてみれば、すべての性格は、DNAと周囲環境によって決まることは明らかだからね。
Diana:	Yeah, that's true, but isn't it a better way to start a conversation with **strangers** than talking about the weather?	ええ、そうなのよ。でも、見知らぬ人と会話を始めるのに、天気について話すよりもより良い方法じゃない？
John:	Yeah. I admit it's a good means to start a conversation with others. But, we have to **take into consideration** the fact that science doesn't support a link between blood type and character.	そうだね。他の人と会話を始めるのには良い手段だと認めるよ。でも、血液型と性格の関係は、科学的には証明されていない事実を考慮に入れなければいけないよ。
Diana:	You think so? I tend to feel much closer with people of a certain blood type. So, I always fall in love with those who have blood type B. By the way, what's yours?	そう思う？私はある特定の血液型の人に対してずっと親しみを感じる傾向にあるの。だから、B型の人といつも恋に落ちるの。ところで、あなたは何型なの？

ケース26　血液型と性格との関係の是非

John: I'm relieved to hear that—mine is A!

> それを聞いて安心したよ。僕はA型だよ。

Words & Phrases

- believe it or not　信じられないような話ですが
- popular　人気がある
- character　性格
- blood type　血液型
- so far　今までのところ
- best-selling series of books　ベストセラーの本
- believe in ～　～の存在を（正確に）信じる
- judge　～を判断する
- for the first time　初めて
- vampire　吸血鬼
- similar　よく似た
- confusing　とまどう
- realistic　現実的な
- determine　～を決定する
- DNA　デオキシリボ核酸
- surrounding environment　周囲環境
- stranger　知らない人、他人
- take ～ into consideration　～を考慮に入れる
- be relieved to ～　～して安心する

Tips　よく使われる表現―感想・判断①―

☐ on second thought
　（よく考えてみると）
☐ come to think of it
　（考えてみると）
☐ on further reflection
　（さらによく考えてみると）
☐ in one's considered opinion
　（いろいろ検討してみた上では）

◆その他の表現

☐ a survey says, that's true, but 〜
　（調査によれば、それは本当だけど、〜）
☐ Do you believe in it?
　（それを信じているの？）
☐ Science doesn't support a link between blood type and character.
　（科学は血液と性格との間の関係を証明していない。）

ケース26　血液型と性格との関係の是非

◆すぐに使える表現　Possible Opinions

- I don't believe in any kind of fortune-telling based on blood type.
  （血液型に基づくいかなる類の占いも信じない。）
- Blood type B can be very goal-oriented and often complete ambitious tasks set before them.
  （血液型Bは非常に目的がハッキリしていて、目の前の大がかりな仕事をこなしてしまう。）
- Blood type fortune-telling is often featured in magazines.
  （血液型に基づく占いが雑誌に特集を組まれる。）
- Descriptions of my character in books on blood type don't match my real character.
  （血液型に関する本の中で、自分の性格に関する説明が実際の性格と合わない。）
- Some people try to adjust themselves to the description of a certain blood type
  （自分自身をある血液型の描写に合わせようとする人がいる。）

ケース27 女性に関する昇進の壁を破る方法

Track 27　How to break the glass ceiling concerning women

⁉ 女性の社会進出が求められているが、女性という理由や結婚、出産、育児などの理由による昇進の壁が存在する。どうすれば昇進の壁を破ることができるのだろうか。

ダイアローグ
Dialogue

TV anchor: There used to be a **glass ceiling regarding** the **presidency**; **that is**, an **invisible barrier preventing** a black or female president. In 2009, Barack Obama **made history** as the first black president of the U.S. **The focus of** the next election may **be** on a woman breaking the glass ceiling.

> 大統領職に関しては、かつてガラスの天井があったものです。つまり、黒人や女性が大統領になるのを妨げる目に見えない壁です。2009年、バラクオバマが、アメリカ合衆国初の黒人大統領として歴史的偉業を成し遂げました。次の選挙の焦点は、ガラスの天井を破る1人の女性かもしれません。

John: Do you feel that there is **currently** a glass ceiling for women?

> 現在は女性に対して、ガラスの天井が存在すると感じるかな？

ケース27 女性に関する昇進の壁を破る方法

Diana: Yes. Under **the Constitution** we are **treated equally**, right? But, the **ratio** of male to female CEOs in **major corporations** is clearly **disproportionate**. Why is that?

ええ。憲法の下、私たちは平等に扱われているのよね。でも、大企業において男性と女性 CEO の比率は、明らかに不均衡よね。それはなぜなの？

John: I hate to say it, but isn't it because women **tend to take a lot of time off**?

言いたくないけど、それは女性が多く休みを取る傾向にあるためかな。

Diana: Are you talking about women's **leaves for maternity** and other **family-related reasons**? It's very hard for women to work while raising children. If that is the main reason, the government should **take the initiative in** breaking the glass ceiling.

あなたは、産休や他の家族に関する理由で取得する女性休暇のことについて言っているの？女性が子供を育てながら働くのは、本当に厳しいのよ。もしそれが、主な理由だとしたら、政府は率先してガラスの天井を破るべきだわ。

John: How? So far, the government has worked hard to create a better working environment for women by **offering** maternity leave, **flextime policies** and so on.

どうやって。今まで、政府は産休、フレックスタイム政策などを提供することで、女性にとってより良い職場環境を作ろうと一生懸命働きかけてきているよ。

Diana: Those policies are not enough.

それらの政策だけでは十分じゃないわ。

John: I know, but what should be done? Could you be more specific?

知っているよ。でも、何がされるべきなの。もっと詳しく話してもらえる？

Diana: Well, I have two ideas on the matter. The first one is **transparency** like glass; there should be no hidden agenda. This is necessary in the **evaluation process**. Today, women

そうね。その問題について2つ考えがあるわ。1つ目はガラスのような透明性ね。つまり、隠された意図はなしでね。これは評価の過程においては必要よ。今日、女性はほぼ

139

have almost the same **academic achievements, ambitions** and **commitment** to their careers as men. I wish that all companies would adopt a system to **evaluate the performance of employees** equally. The second one is **encouragement**. I mean the government should encourage companies to **make the most of** women's **talents** and experiences as **consumers**, mothers, wives **and so forth**.

男性と同じような学力、仕事に対する野心や献身を有しているわ。すべての企業が従業員の業績を平等に評価するシステムを導入すればいいのに。2つ目は奨励ね。つまり政府は企業に消費者、母、妻などとしての女性の能力や経験を最大限活用するように奨励すべきだわ。

Words & Phrases

- glass ceiling　目に見ない障害、壁
- regarding　〜に関して、〜について
- presidency　大統領の地位
- that is　すなわち
- invisible barrier　目に見えないバリア
- prevent　〜を妨げる
- make history　歴史的な偉業を成し遂げる
- the focus of 〜 is …　〜の焦点は…である
- currently　現在は
- the Constitution　憲法
- treat　〜を扱う
- ratio　割合、比率
- major corporation　大企業
- disproportionate　不均衡な
- tend to 〜　〜する傾向がある
- take a lot of time off　多く休みをとる
- leaves for maternity　産休
- family-related reason　家族に関係した理由
- take the initiative in 〜　〜を率先してやる
- offer　〜を提示する、〜を提供する
- flextime policy　フレックスタイム政策
- transparency　透明性
- evaluation process　評価の過程
- academic achievement　学力
- ambition　熱意、野心
- commitment　献身
- evaluate the performance of employees　従業員の業績を評価する
- encouragement　激励
- make the most of 〜　〜を最大限に活用する
- talent　才能
- consumer　消費者
- and so forth　〜など

Tips　よく使われる表現—提案②—

- ☐ **I have two ideas on the matter.**
  （その問題について 2 つ考えがある。）
- ☐ **I have two ideas concerning your opinion.**
  （君の意見について 2 つ考えがある。）
- ☐ **I have a couple of ideas about your idea.**
  （君の考えについて 2、3 考えがある。）
- ☐ **There are two ideas on the issue.**
  （その問題について 2 つ考えがある。）

◆その他の表現

- Why is that?
  (それはどうしてなの？)
- I hate to say it, but 〜
  (言いたくないけど、〜)
- if that is the main reason, 〜
  (もしそれが主な理由なら、〜)
- Could you be more specific?
  (もっと詳しく話していただけませんか。)

◆すぐに使える表現　Possible Opinions

- The president in Finland was a woman.
  (フィンランドの大統領は女性だった。)
- Equal academic achievements don't guarantee fair opportunities.
  (等しい学力は公平なチャンスを保障しない。)
- Generally speaking, women have lower incomes than men.
  (一般的に言って、女性は男性より所得が低い。)
- There are conscious and unconscious biases towards women.
  (女性に対して、意識的または無意識的な偏見がある。)
- All people should be treated equally regardless of race, gender or skin color.
  (すべての人種、性、肌の色にかかわらず、人々は平等に扱われるべきである。)

ケース 28 笑いの力を効果的に利用する方法
Track 28　How to effectively harness the power of laughter

笑いがストレスを解消し、病気の予防や治療においても効果を発揮すると言われる。どうすれば笑いの力を向上させることができるだろうか。

ダイアローグ
Dialogue

TV anchor: Past studies suggest that laughing **increases resistance to** disease and helps **keep** people **fit.** To put it another way, laughter is **effective** in **maintaining the proper functioning** of the **immune system. Experts** around the world have started to **utilize** laughter as part of their **treatments.**

これまでの研究によれば、笑いは、病気への抵抗力を向上させたり、人々が健康を保つのに役立つとのことです。別の言い方をすれば、笑いは、免疫システムの適切な機能を維持するのに効果的なのです。世界中の専門家は笑いを治療の一部として活用し始めています。

John: That sounds interesting. Didn't you say your uncle gets tired with his job, **faces tough**

それは興味深いね。君の叔父は仕事で疲れ、大変な時期に直面していて、

143

	times and becomes stressed?	ストレスを抱えているって言っていたね。
Diana:	Yeah, after having made a big mistake on the job, he can't **concentrate** well at work.	そうなの。仕事でミスを犯してから、仕事に集中できないみたい。
John:	Don't you think this idea can help him in some way?	この考えが、彼を助けるのにどうにか役に立つと思わない？
Diana:	What do you mean?	どういう意味？
John:	**Making a mistake** at work may mean he failed on the job, but not as a person. As human beings, failure in life is **unavoidable**; people make mistakes. Besides, there are some **pessimistic** people who become **negative** soon after they've **failed** in some way. Nobody admires such negativity. Your uncle shouldn't take it so seriously. I'm sure his mistake will lead to a big **success** some day. Right?	仕事でミスを犯すことは、仕事での失敗を意味するかもしれないね。でも、人として失敗した訳じゃない。人として人生における失敗は避けられないね。人は失敗するものなんだ。しかも、なんらかの理由で失敗した後すぐに否定的になってしまう悲観的な人々がいるよね。そのような消極的な態度を好む人はいないよね。彼は、ミスをそれ程深刻に受け止めるべきじゃないんだ。きっと、彼のミスはいつか大きな成功につながるよ。そうだろう。
Diana:	It's possible. So, what should he do now?	その可能性はあるわね。で、彼は今どうすべきなの？
John:	Your uncle needs to change his attitude first. He should **take time to go out** and do something he enjoys. All he needs is the **courage** to laugh at his mistake, and he will have a **brighter** future.	君の叔父は、まず態度を変える必要があるよ。彼は、時間をとって外出して何か楽しむべきだよ。彼に必要なのは、自分の失敗を笑う勇気だね。そうすれば、彼には明るい未来が待っているよ。
Diana:	You're absolutely right. If he did that, he	まったくその通りよ。も

would become **optimistic**. They say laughter is the best medicine, and, best of all, it's free. Some day, I hope doctors will start **prescribing** laughter.

し彼がそうすれば、楽観的になれるわ。笑いは百薬の長と言うわ。とりわけ、タダでしょう。いつかドクターが笑いの処方を始める日が来ると良いね。

Words & Phrases

- ☐ harness　〜を利用する
- ☐ increases resistance to 〜　〜への抵抗力を向上させる
- ☐ keep 〜 fit　〜を健康に保つ
- ☐ effective　効果的な
- ☐ maintain the proper functioning　適切な機能を維持する
- ☐ immune system　免疫システム
- ☐ expert　専門家
- ☐ utilize　〜を利用する
- ☐ treatment　治療
- ☐ face tough times　大切な時期に直面する
- ☐ concentrate (on 〜)　(〜に)集中する
- ☐ make a mistake　間違いをする
- ☐ unavoidable　避けられない
- ☐ pessimistic　悲観的な
- ☐ negative　否定的な
- ☐ fail　失敗する
- ☐ success　成功
- ☐ take time to go out　時間をとって外出する
- ☐ courage　勇気
- ☐ bright　明るい
- ☐ optimistic　楽観的な
- ☐ prescribe　〜を処方する

Tips　よく使われる表現—言い換え①—

- [ ] to put it another way
   （別の言い方をすれば）
- [ ] that is (to say)
   （換言すると、すなわち）
- [ ] what I mean is 〜
   （つまり〜）
- [ ] to put it differently
   （違う言い方をすれば）

◆その他の表現

- [ ] past studies suggest that 〜
   （過去の研究によれば〜）
- [ ] What do you mean?
   （どういう意味なの？）
- [ ] all he needs is 〜
   （彼に必要なことは〜である）
- [ ] You're absolutely right.
   （まったくその通りである。）

ケース28　笑いの力を効果的に利用する方法

> ◆すぐに使える表現　Possible Opinions

☐ You should learn to laugh at yourself and learn tips to make others laugh.
（自分を笑う方法とほかの人を笑わせるコツを身につけるべきだ。）

☐ Laughter has a positive effect on us and makes us healthier.
（笑いはプラス効果をもたらし、私たちを健康にしてくれる。）

☐ I firmly believe that humor and smiling are the best remedies for sick people.
（ユーモアと笑顔は病気の人々にとって最良の治療法だと確信している。）

☐ Life is short, so there's no time to spend worrying.
（人生は短い。だから心配して過ごす時間なんてない。）

☐ A smile is a secret weapon that can unite people.
（笑顔は人々を結びつける秘密兵器である。）

ケース29 生徒のカンニングを防ぐ方法
How to prevent students' cheating

Track 29

コピー&ペーストが一般化し、コピペ判定ツールというソフトが作られている。どうすればカンニングやコピペを防ぐことができるのだろうか。

ダイアローグ
Dialogue

TV anchor: In a survey of high schools, almost **three-fourths of** the students admitted to **cheating** on tests. They used smartphones or **hidden notes** specially made for that **purpose**. So, some schools have decided to introduce the **latest technology** in **combating** cheating. The **device captures a full 360-degree image** of the classroom. When the test begins, the device records audio and visual.

高校のある調査では、ほぼ4分の3の生徒が、テストでカンニングをしたことがあると認めました。彼らはスマートフォンやカンニング目的で特別に作った隠しメモを使いました。このため、学校の中にはカンニングに対抗するために最新テクノロジーの導入を決めたところがあります。その装置では、教室の360度の画像が撮れます。テストが始まると、その機械は音声と画像を記録するのです。

ケース29　生徒のカンニングを防ぐ方法

Diana: Wow, it's an **amazing** battle between teachers and students.

わあ、まさに教師と生徒の驚くべき戦いね。

John: I'm **astonished** by the high ratio of students who cheat. This is the result of so many students **growing accustomed to** using computers and smartphones.

カンニングする生徒の割合が高いことに驚いたな。これは、多くの生徒がコンピュータやスマートフォンの扱いに慣れてきた結果だね。

Diana: I know. **In a sense,** they **get paralyzed with** the **convenience** of high-tech devices. They **take it as a matter of course** to **copy and paste large portions of** school reports and **log onto** the Internet to look up test answers.

そうね。ある意味、生徒はハイテク機械の便利さに感覚が麻痺しているわ。彼らは、学校のレポートの大部分をコピーして貼り付けること、テストの答えを調べるためにインターネットにログインすることを、当たり前のことと受け止めているわ。

John: That's right. **It's likely that** they don't even feel guilty about cheating. How can we **prevent** students **from** cheating?

そうだね。彼らは、カンニングについて罪の意識さえ感じていないようだよ。どうすれば、生徒がカンニングするのを防げるだろう。

Diana: First, students should not be allowed to bring devices into school. Second, we need to let them know cheating may lead to **suspension** or **expulsion** from school.

まず、生徒が、機械を学校に持ち込むことを許可しないことね。2つ目に、カンニングで、学校を停学や退学になる可能性があることを彼らに知らせる必要があるわ。

John: But, that won't solve the **fundamental** cause of cheating. How can we show them it's morally wrong to cheat?

でも、それは、カンニングの根本的な原因を解決しないよ。どうすれば、彼らにカンニングすることは道徳的に悪い、と示せるんだろう。

Diana: That's the most difficult part. Even business people **commit fraud** almost every day.

そこは最も難しい部分ね。ビジネスマンだってほぼ毎日不正行為を犯しているんだもの。

John: I've got it. Before teaching not to cheat on tests, we adults need to become good **role-models** for students.

わかった。テストでカンニングしないように教える前に、私たち大人が、生徒の良い手本となる必要があるんだ。

Diana: I like that. I'm all for it.

それ気に入ったわ。それに大賛成よ。

Words & Phrases

- three-fourths of ～　～の4分の3
- cheating　不正行為
- hidden notes　秘密のメモ
- purpose　目的
- latest technology　最新の技術
- combat　～と戦う
- device　機械
- capture　～の画像・映像を撮る
- a full 360-degree image　360度の映像
- amazing　すごい
- astonish　～を驚かす
- grow accustomed to ～ing　～に慣れっこになる
- In a sense　ある意味
- get paralyzed with ～　～に麻痺する
- convenience　便利
- take ～ as a matter of course　～を当然のことと思う
- copy and paste　コピー&ペーストする
- large portion of ～　～の大部分
- log onto ～　～にログインする
- It's likely that ～　～のようである
- prevent ～ from …ing　～が…することを妨げる
- suspension　停学
- expulsion　退学
- fundamental　基本的な
- commit fraud　不正行為をする
- role-model　他人の手本となる人物

ケース29　生徒のカンニングを防ぐ方法

Tips よく使われる表現―賛成①―

☐ I'm all for it.
（それに大賛成である。）
☐ I fully agree with you.
（あなたにまったく同感である。）
☐ You're 100 percent right.
（あなたは100％正しい。）
☐ You're right on the mark.
（あなたは図星である。）
☐ I think you've convinced me.
（あなたは私を納得させました。）

◆その他の表現

☐ in a survey of ～
（～の調査では）
☐ this is the result of ～
（これは～の結果である）
☐ That's right.
（そのとおりです。）
☐ That's the most difficult part.
（最も難しい部分である。）
☐ I've got it.
（わかりました。）

◆すぐに使える表現　Possible Opinions

- [ ] Cheating on an exam is not a crime, but accessing someone's computer system is a crime.
(試験でのカンニングは犯罪ではない。しかし誰かのコンピュータシステムにアクセスすることは犯罪である。)
- [ ] Reporting dishonesty anonymously is a good system.
(不正を匿名で通報することは良いシステムである。)
- [ ] Students should spend their time studying for tests rather than studying how to cheat on them.
(生徒はテストでカンニングする方法を研究するよりも、むしろテストのために勉強することに時間を費やすべきである。)
- [ ] In the case of a student being caught cheating, the test will be invalidated.
(生徒がカンニングしているのを見つけられた場合、テストは無効になる。)

ケース30 若さを保つ方法
How to keep ourselves young

Track 30

年齢には、実年齢、精神年齢と肉体年齢の3つあるという。どうすれば若さを保てるのだろうか。

ダイアローグ
Dialogue

TV anchor: It's difficult to **define** what youth is. The **poet** Samuel Ullman said, "Youth is not a time of life—it is a **state of mind**; it is a **temper** of the will, a quality of the imagination…. Nobody grows old by **merely** living a number of years; people grow old only by **deserting their ideals**."

青春を定義することは難しいです。詩人のサミュエルウルマンは「青春とは、人生のある期間ではなく、心の持ち方をいう。たくましい意志、ゆたかな創造力…、年を重ねただけでは、人は老いない。理想を失う時に初めて老いる。」と述べています。

John: What do you think of his poem?

この詩をどう思う？

153

Diana: Well, **to tell you the truth**, the older I get, the less **curious** I become, and my energy **decreases**. So his words **resonate with** me.

そうね。実を言えば、年をとるにつれて、好奇心がなくなり、エネルギーも少なくなっているわ。だから彼の言葉は私の心に響くわ。

John: I feel the same. The fact is that we are getting older every day, so we need to learn how to keep ourselves young at heart.

僕も同じだよ。実は、私たちは毎日年をとってるんだ。だから心を若く維持する秘訣を学ぶ必要があるんだ。

Diana: You got that right. But how?

その通りよ。でも、どうやって？

John: Actually, no one can tell us what to do, so we need to **change our own attitude**. First, we should try something new and fun every day. Second, **don't put off till tomorrow what we can do today**. Third, don't be **pessimistic**. Fourth, find our **favorite** things and do what we love.

実際には、だれもやり方を教えてはくれないんだ。だから、自分たちの態度を変える必要があるんだ。最初に毎日新しい楽しいことに挑戦するべきだね。2つ目に今日できることは明日まで延期しない。3つ目に悲観的になってはいけない。4つ目に好きなことを見つけて、好きなことをすることだね。

Diana: I don't know **whether** they are all possible. But **to some extent**, I'd like to keep them in mind. What else?

それらをすべてこなせるかどうかわからないわ。でも、ある程度、心に留めておくわ。ほかには？

John: Last but not least, remember that age is just a number. It doesn't matter that much. What matters in life is to remain young **in spirit**. Then we can stay **mentally** young although we are **physically** aging.

最後だけど大切なことは、年齢が単なる数字だということを覚えておいて。年齢はそれ程重要じゃないんだ。人生で最も大切なことは、精神的に若くあり続けることなんだ。そうすれば、肉体的に老いても、精神的に若くしていられるんだ。

Diana: Hearing this, I feel like my strength has been

これを聞いていたら、力

renewed. Besides, I think older people with a young spirit look cooler than younger people with an old spirit.

が回復してきたような気がするわ。しかも、若い精神をもった年配の人は、年老いた精神を持つ若者と比べて、ずっと格好良く見えると思うわ。

Words & Phrases

- define ～を定義する
- poet 詩人
- state of mind 精神状態
- temper 気分、短気
- merely ただ単に
- desert one's ideal 理想・目標を捨てる
- to tell you the truth 実を言えば
- curious 好奇心の強い
- decrease 減る
- resonate with ～ ～の心に響く
- change one's attitude 態度を変える
- Don't put off till tomorrow what we can do today. 今日できることを明日に延期するな。
- pessimistic 悲観的な
- favorite 大好きな
- whether ～かどうか
- to some extent ある程度
- in spirit 気持ちの上では、心では
- mentally 精神的に
- physically 身体的に
- renew ～を取り戻す、～を回復する

Tips　よく使われる表現―賛成②―

☐ You got that right.
　（その通りである。）
☐ That's exactly what I think.
　（私の考えも全くその通りである。）
☐ That's just what I was thinking.
　（それがまさに私が考えていたことである。）
☐ You're absolutely right.
　（全くその通りである。）
☐ You've said it.
　（全くその通りである。）

◆その他の表現

☐ What do you think of his poem?
　（彼の詩についてどう思う？）
☐ I feel the same.
　（同じように思う。）
☐ the fact is that ～
　（実は、～である）
☐ last but not least
　（大事なことをひとつ言い残したが）
☐ what matters in life is to ～
　（人生で大切なことは～である）

ケース30　若さを保つ方法

◆すぐに使える表現　Possible Opinions

☐ Live your life to the fullest because you never know when it might end.
（精一杯人生を生きなさい。人生がいつ終わるかわからないのだから。）

☐ Being optimistic is the best way to keep ourselves young.
（楽観的でいることが若さを保つ最も良い方法である。）

☐ People are as young as their hope, as old as their despair.
（人々は希望と共に若く、絶望と共に老いる。）

☐ Everybody has a tomorrow; tomorrow is a new day for everybody.
（誰にも明日がある。明日はみんなにとって新しい一日である。）

☐ Seize the day.
（今を生きよ。）

ケース 31 子供のテレビ視聴時間の制限方法

Track 31

How to limit children's TV viewing

テレビを見ると家族間のコミュニケーションが少なくなる。どうすればテレビ視聴時間の制限ができるのだろうか。

ダイアローグ
Dialogue

TV anchor: According to a survey, "Children are getting weaker, **clumsier** and more easily tired. It's because they eat breakfast less **frequently**, play less sports and spend more time watching TV."

ある調査によれば、子供たちはよりひ弱に、不器用に、そして疲れやすくなっているといいます。それは、朝食をとる回数が減り、スポーツを以前ほどしなくなり、テレビの視聴時間が増えているためです。

John: What do you think of this issue?

この問題をどう思う？

Diana: This is **probably** due to a **vicious cycle**.

これはおそらく悪循環のせいね。

ケース31　子供のテレビ視聴時間の制限方法

John: What do you mean by a vicious cycle?

悪循環ってどういう意味なの？

Diana: Well, children don't play outside enough **after school**, so they don't feel tired at night and **stay up late** watching TV. As a result, they feel sleepy in the morning and they **tend to** eat breakfast less often or **skip** it.

ええ。子供たちは放課後十分に外で遊ばないわ。だから、夜、疲れを感じないのよ。それでテレビを見て夜更かしするの。結果として、彼らは、朝眠気を感じて、朝食をあまり取らなかったり、抜いたりするの。

John: Then, how can they break the cycle?

それでは、どうすればその悪循環を断つことができるの？

Diana: I'm sure the time spent watching TV is the key. As the survey says, too much **exposure to TV has a negative influence on** children. Therefore, they should limit their time watching TV. If children do this, it will **have positive effects on** them.

テレビを視聴して過ごす時間が鍵ね。調査が示すように、長時間にわたるテレビ視聴は、子供に悪影響を及ぼすのよ。だから、子供たちはテレビを見る時間を制限すべきなの。そうすれば子供たちにはプラス効果を及ぼすわ。

John: What are these positive effects?

プラス効果って何？

Diana: I'm sure less TV viewing would increase time for **conversation** between children and parents. More time for conversation would give the family a chance to relax and **enjoy each other's company**. Also, people would become more **creative** in such an environment by having more time for **hands-on activities** like arts and crafts. Most people would come to **realize** the merits of not watching TV. That's the start of a **positive cycle**. However

テレビの視聴時間が短いと、子供と両親との間の会話時間が増えるわ。会話の時間が増えれば、家族がリラックスしたり団らんする機会が多くなるわ。また、人々はそのような環境では、工芸などの体験活動をする時間が増えて、より創造的になれるわ。ほとんどの人はテレビを視聴しないことのメリットに気づくようになるわ。それがよい循環の始まりなの。でも、言うは易く、行うは難しだわ。問題は誰が最初にテレビのスイッチを切るかよ。

it's easier said than done. The problem is who will start **turning off** the TV.

Words & Phrases

- clumsy （人や動きが）不器用な
- frequently 頻繁に
- probably 十中八九は、おそらく
- vicious cycle 悪循環
- after school 放課後
- stay up late 夜更かしをする
- tend to 〜 〜する傾向がある
- skip 〜を抜かす、〜を省略する
- exposure 〜にふれること
- have a negative influence on 〜 〜に悪影響を与える
- have a positive effect on 〜 〜に良い影響を与える
- conversation 会話
- enjoy each other's company 和気あいあいと楽しむ
- creative 創造力がある
- hands-on activities 体験活動
- realize 〜に気づく
- positive cycle 良い循環、好循環
- it's easier said than done. 口にするのは簡単だが、実行するのは難しい。
- turn off 〜 〜を消す

ケース31　子供のテレビ視聴時間の制限方法

Tips　よく使われる表現—結果—

☐ as a result
　（結果として）
☐ consequently
　（その結果として）
☐ therefore
　（それゆえに）
☐ thus
　（それゆえに）
☐ accordingly
　（その結果）
☐ in conclusion
　（結論として）

◆その他の表現

☐ according to a survey
　（ある調査によると）
☐ What do you think of this issue?
　（この問題についてどう思うの？）
☐ due to 〜
　（〜が原因で）
☐ What do you mean by a vicious cycle?
　（悪循環ってどういう意味なの？）
☐ as the survey says
　（その調査が示すように）
☐ also
　（さらに）
☐ however
　（しかし）

☐ the problem is 〜
(問題は〜である)

◆すぐに使える表現　Possible Opinions

☐ There's too much violence and sex on TV these days.
(最近、テレビにはあまりにも多くの暴力とセックスがあふれている。)
☐ TV brings us information, education and entertainment as well in a variety of ways.
(テレビは、様々な方法で、情報、教育、娯楽をもたらす。)
☐ If we watched less TV, we would spend more time reading.
(もし私たちが、テレビの視聴を減らせば、読書により多くの時間を費やすであろう。)
☐ In the USA, there is screen-free week where people are encouraged to turn off the screens of TVs, computers and hand-held devices.
(アメリカ合衆国では、人々がテレビ、コンピュータ、携帯機器の画面を切ることが奨励されるスクリーンフリー週間がある。)

ケース32 個々のネチケットを確立する方法
Track 32　How to establish the netiquette of each individual

インターネット上の、基本的なルールや、掲示板等の利用規約など、利用者間のネチケットがある。どうすればネチケットを身につけることができるのだろうか。

ダイアローグ
Dialogue

TV anchor: The number of **vicious** messages **attacking certain** blogs **is on the rise**. It's difficult to find out who **posts** these messages. Therefore, a lot of **unfounded rumors** are being posted by **anonymous users**. Some blogs **targeted** by these **irresponsible** messages have **been forced to** shut down. In January, 10 people were arrested **on suspicion of** posting vicious messages on blogs.

ある特定のブログを攻撃する悪意あるメッセージの数が増えています。これらのメッセージを誰が投稿したかを見つけるのは困難です。そのため、たくさんの根も葉もない噂が匿名のユーザーから投稿されています。これらの無責任なメッセージに標的にされたいくつかのブログは、閉鎖せざるを得ませんでした。1月には10人の人々がブログに悪意あるメッセージを投稿した疑いで逮捕されました。

John: This kind of attack against a blog is called **flaming**. Someone posts unfounded rumors and readers keep posting more messages **in response to** them. In that way, unfounded rumors spread like flames. Particularly bad rumors spread the fastest. **In the end**, they cause big problems. Actually, an actress **killed herself** because she became the target of unfounded rumors.

この種のブログへの攻撃は炎上と呼ばれているんだ。誰かが根も葉もない噂を投稿して、読者がその噂に応えてより多くのメッセージを投稿し続けるんだ。そのようにして、根も葉もない噂が、炎のように広がるんだ。特に悪い噂はすぐに広がるんだ。結局、それらの噂が大きな問題を引き起こすんだ。実際に、ある女優は、根も葉もない噂の標的になったために自殺したんだ。

Diana: Yeah. She must have received hundreds of messages on her blog every day. I'm sure she couldn't **bear** the rumors any more.

そうね。彼女は、毎日ブログに何百というメッセージを受け取ったに違いないわ。きっと彼女は噂にもうこれ以上耐えられなかったのよ。

John: I think so too. How could we **prevent** such flaming?

そう思うね。どうすればそんな炎上を防げるだろうか。

Diana: Why don't we teach children at home and in school the **potential dangers** of careless Internet use? At least, we should teach them basic **netiquette**. For instance, they should **pay** more **attention to** what they write. They also should have the ability to judge whether messages they read are true or not.

子供たちにインターネットの不注意な利用の潜在的危険性について、家庭や学校で、教えたらどうかしら。少なくとも、私たちは、子供たちに基本的なネチケットは教えるべきよ。例えば、子供たちは自分たちの書くことにもっと注意を払うべきよ。また、子供たちは、目にするメッセージが本当かどうか判断する能力を身につけるべきね。

John: I agree with you 100%. These days, children tend to misunderstand the meaning of freedom of speech, because **with freedom comes responsibility**. So, children should read their

100％君に賛成だよ。最近、子供たちは、言論の自由の意味を誤解する傾向にあるんだ。自由には責任が伴っているんだから。そのため、メッセージを投稿する前に注意深く読むべきなんだ。また、

> own messages carefully before posting them. Also, children should learn to look at their messages from a reader's point of view.

読者の視点に立って自分のメッセージを読むことを学ぶべきなんだ。

Diana: In that way, they will learn netiquette.

そうやって、ネチケットを学ぶのね。

John: Yeah, they **can't be too careful** in posting messages.

そうだね。メッセージを投稿する際には、いくら注意してもし過ぎることはないね。

Diana: Yeah, just one **click** could cause a **drastic change** in somebody's life.

そうね。たった一度のクリックで誰かの人生を劇的に変化させてしまうかもしれないからね。

Words & Phrases

- vicious messages　悪意あるメッセージ
- attack　～を攻撃する、～を非難する
- certain　ある
- be on the rise　増えている
- post　（情報を）投稿する
- unfounded rumor　根も葉もない噂
- anonymous user　匿名のユーザー
- target　～を標的とする、～を狙う
- irresponsible　無責任な
- be forced to ～　～せざるを得ない
- on suspicion of ～　～の疑いで
- flaming　フレーミング、ネット上での中傷
- in response to ～　～に応えて
- in the end　結局
- kill oneself　自殺する
- bear　～に耐える
- prevent　～を妨げる
- potential danger　潜在的危険性
- netiquette　ネット上のエチケット
- pay attention to ～　～に注意を払う
- with freedom comes responsibility　自由には責任が伴う
- can't be too careful　用心するにこしたことはない
- click　クリック
- drastic change　劇的変化

Tips よく使われる表現—観点②—

- from a reader's point of view
  （読者の観点から）
- economically speaking
  （経済的に言えば）
- scientifically speaking
  （科学的に言えば）
- from an economic point of view
  （経済的視点から）
- from a global point of view
  （グローバル的視点から）
- from a scientific point of view
  （科学的視点から）

◆その他の表現

- therefore
  （それゆえに、だから）
- in the end
  （結局）
- cause
  （〜を引き起こす）
- I think so too.
  （私もそう思う。）
- for instance
  （例えば）
- I agree with you 100%.
  （あなたと100％同じ意見である。）

ケース32　個々のネチケットを確立する方法

◆すぐに使える表現　Possible Opinions

- ☐ It's natural to regulate vicious behavior.
  （悪意ある行動を規制するのは当然である。）
- ☐ Users can hide themselves behind the anonymity of the Internet.
  （ユーザーはインターネットの匿名性の背後に隠れることができる。）
- ☐ Surfing the Internet is addictive.
  （インターネットサーフィンには中毒性がある。）
- ☐ There is freedom of speech on the Internet.
  （インターネット上には言論の自由がある。）
- ☐ Censoring anything seen as offensive could lead to violating the freedom of speech.
  （攻撃的だと見なされるものを検閲することは、言論の自由を侵害することにつながる。）
- ☐ Some people only post negative comments to evoke a response.
  （反応を得るために、否定的なコメントしか投稿しない人々がいる。）

ケース33　地震の防災対策
Track 33　How to prepare for earthquakes

❓ 怖いものの代表を地震・雷・火事・親父という。どうすれば地震の防災対策ができるのだろうか。

ダイアローグ
Dialogue

TV anchor: According to the earthquake research committee, **preventative home measures** against earthquakes are still **insufficient**. About 60% of earthquake **injuries** are caused by **fallen furniture**, and broken glass and dishes. Surprisingly enough, it's **estimated** that about 40% of people don't fix furniture to walls or ceilings **in preparation for** an earthquake.

地震調査委員会によると、家庭の予防策は、まだ不十分です。地震の負傷の約60％は、倒れた家具、壊れたガラスや食器が原因で起こっています。驚くべきことに、地震に備えて約40％もの人々が、家具を壁や天井に固定していないのです。

ケース33　地震の防災対策

John: Have you taken any measures to **prepare for** big earthquakes?

大地震に備えて何か対策をとっているの？

Diana: Yeah. I **fastened** all my furniture to the walls with **L-shaped metal brackets** and **screws**. Many people **overlook** that big **cupboards** and TV sets could suddenly become **deadly weapons** during big earthquakes. Besides, L-shaped metal brackets and screws are very cheap preventative measures.

ええ。私はL字型の家具転倒防止金具とネジで、すべての家具を壁に固定したわ。大地震で大きな食器棚やテレビセットが突然凶器になることを、多くの人々が見落としているのよ。それに、L字型の家具転倒防止金具とネジはとても安い予防策よ。

John: I have never thought of doing something like that.

僕は、そのようなことするなんて考えてもみなかったよ。

Diana: **You must be kidding.** Natural **disasters** such as typhoons and earthquakes wait for no one. **To make matters worse**, earthquakes are **unpredictable**.

冗談でしょう。台風や地震のような自然災害は、待ってはくれないの。さらに悪い事に、地震は予想不可能でしょう。

John: You're absolutely right. Besides that, what sort of preventative measures should we take?

全くその通りだね。それ以外に、どんな種類の予防策を、取るべきかな？

Diana: I think there are three types of preventative measures. They are governmental preparation, **mutual** communal preparation and careful **individual** preparation. I'm sure the last one is the most important.

3つのタイプの予防策があると思うわ。それらは、政府の準備、コミュニティーの相互援助の準備、そして入念な個人準備だわ。きっと最後の準備が最も大切だわ。

John: So, individually what can I do to **lessen**

それで、地震の被害を減らすために、個人的に何

earthquake **damage**? ができるかな。

Diana: Well, first, find the safest place in the house. Next, prepare **emergency supplies** in a **backpack** such as **non-perishable foods**, drinking water, emergency medicine, a **portable** radio and so on. If an earthquake strikes, calm down, protect your head and **duck** under a table. Then **extinguish** all fires. We can't prevent an earthquake, but if we take every possible step in **securing** our homes, we can **limit** earthquake **damage**.

そうね。最初に、家の中で最も安全な場所を見つけることね。次に、リュックサックの中に例えば、保存の利く食べ物、飲み水、緊急用の薬、携帯用ラジオなどの非常時の生活必需品を用意することね。もし地震が発生したら、落ち着いて、頭を保護し、テーブルの下にかがむの。それから、すべての火は消してね。地震は防ぐことはできないけど、もし私たちが家を守る点で、ありとあらゆる手段を講じれば、地震の被害を抑えることが可能なの。

ケース33　地震の防災対策

Words & Phrases

- preventative home measures　家庭の予防策
- insufficient　不十分な、足りない
- injury　けが
- fallen furniture　倒れた家具
- estimate　〜だと見積もる、〜を評価する
- in preparation for 〜　〜に備えて
- prepare for 〜　〜のために準備する
- fasten　〜を固定する
- L-shaped metal bracket　L字型の家具取付金属
- screw　ネジ
- overlook　〜を見落とす
- cupboard　食器棚
- deadly weapon　凶器
- You must be kidding.　冗談でしょう。
- disaster　大災害
- to make matters worse　さらに悪い事に
- unpredictable　予測できない
- mutual　相互の
- individual　個人の、個々の
- lessen damage　被害を減らす
- emergency supplies　非常時の生活必需品
- backpack　リュックサック
- non-perishable foods　保存の利く食料品
- portable　携帯用の
- duck　かがむ
- extinguish　〜を消す
- secure　〜を守る
- limit damage　被害を抑える

Tips　よく使われる表現―感想・判断②―

- surprisingly enough
  （驚くべきことに）
- interestingly enough
  （大変興味深いことに）
- it is regrettable that 〜
  （〜は残念なことである）
- it is reasonable to think that 〜
  （〜と考えるのは妥当である）
- it is appropriate to say that 〜
  （〜と言うのは適切である）

◆その他の表現

- according to the earthquake research committee
  (地震調査委員会によれば)
- be caused by ～
  (～に起因する)
- have you taken any measures to ～?
  (～するため、なんらかの対策をとっていますか)
- You're absolutely right.
  (あなたが絶対に正しい。)
- besides that
  (その他に)

◆すぐに使える表現　Possible Opinions

- We should keep three days' supply of food and water stored at home.
  (私たちは3日分の食べ物と水を家に保管すべきである。)
- We need to build earthquake-resistant buildings.
  (私たちは耐震の住宅を建てる必要がある。)
- When you are near the ocean, run to a high area as soon as possible in case of ocean waves.
  (あなたが海の近くにいる時には、津波に備えてできるだけ早く高い場所へ走りなさい。)
- We are required to participate in disaster drills.
  (私たちには防災訓練に参加することが求められる。)
- It's important to increase the number of evacuation shelters such as hospitals and schools.
  (病院や学校などの避難場所の数を増やすことが重要である。)

ケース34 献血者の数を増やす方法

Track 34　How to increase the number of blood donors

献血は一定の条件を満たせば、誰でもできる社会貢献である。献血の量が増えない原因は何だろうか。

ダイアローグ
Dialogue

TV Anchor: **Millions of** people need **blood transfusions**, but the number of **blood donors** has been decreasing. We're facing a **looming blood shortage**. The **declining** number of donors **in their teens** and 20s is **particularly** worrying.

何百万人もの人が輸血を必要としています。しかし献血者の数が減っています。私たちは、迫りくる血液不足に直面しています。10代と20代の献血者の減少が特に心配です。

Diana: Have you donated blood?

今までに献血したことある？

John: Me? Yeah. Actually, I'm a regular blood

僕？あるよ。実際、僕は

donor. I'm **making a contribution to** society through blood donation. Giving blood is a very simple thing to do, but not everybody wants to donate their blood.

Diana: I have never donated blood for two reasons. First, I don't like the pain of **syringes**.

John: What is the second reason?

Diana: I have low blood pressure. Simply taking blood to do a blood test makes me **dizzy**. I **am** not **opposed to** the idea of blood donation. I just can't do it.

John: Yours is a **rare case**. According to the survey, one in four of those who haven't donated said they didn't know about the looming blood shortage. So, **the Red Cross Society** should make an effort to inform people about the problem.

Diana: I agree with you. Donating blood is a **volunteer activity**. Therefore, once people are motivated to donate blood, won't the number of donors increase?

John: Yes. Moreover, donating blood **has a big advantage**. It's like a free **health screening**.

In 10 days, you will receive **detailed information** regarding your blood. It includes information about **blood pressure**, possible **liver** problems and so on. This way, blood donation not only saves lives, but also is a way for donors to get a **medical check-up**.

10日後には、自分の血液に関する詳細な情報を受け取れるんだ。血圧、起こりうる肝機能障害などの情報が含まれているんだ。このように献血は命を救うだけでなく、献血者にとって健康診断を受ける方法の一つでもあるんだ。

Words & Phrases

- millions of 〜　多数の〜、何百万という〜
- blood transfusion　輸血
- blood donor　献血者
- looming　迫り来る、すぐ起こりそうだ
- blood shortage　血液不足
- declining　低下している
- in one's teens　10代で
- particularly　特に
- make a contribution to 〜　〜に貢献する、〜に寄与する
- syringe　皮下注射器
- dizzy　目まいがする、ふらふらする
- be opposed to 〜　〜に反対である
- rare case　珍しいケース
- the Red Cross Society　赤十字社
- volunteer activity　ボランティア活動
- have a big advantage　大きな利点がある
- health screening　人間ドック
- detailed information　詳細な情報
- blood pressure　血圧
- liver　肝臓
- medical check-up　健康診断、人間ドック

Tips　よく使われる表現―賛成③―

- [ ] I agree with you.
    （あなたに賛成である。）
- [ ] I share the same view.
    （あなたと同意見である。）
- [ ] I feel the same way.
    （私も同感である。）
- [ ] I am with you.
    （あなたに賛成である。）
- [ ] I couldn't agree more.
    （あなたに大賛成である。）

◆その他の表現

- [ ] What is the second reason?
    （2つ目の理由は何なの？）
- [ ] I am not opposed to the idea of blood donation.
    （私は献血の考え方に反対していない。）
- [ ] according to the survey
    （その調査によれば）
- [ ] therefore
    （それゆえに、したがって）
- [ ] moreover
    （さらに）

ケース34　献血者の数を増やす方法

◆すぐに使える表現　Possible Opinions

☐ It's necessary to improve services for donors, such as providing them with transportation fees.
（交通費を提供するなど、献血者に対するサービスを改善することが必要である。）

☐ We should set up an organization or award to motivate repeat donors.
（私たちは、常連の献血者をその気にさせるため組織や賞を設けるべきである。）

☐ One way to increase the number of regular donors is to raise public awareness about the need for blood donation.
（常連の献血者の数を増やす方法の一つは、献血の必要性についての国民意識を高めることである。）

☐ We need to increase donation opportunities.
（献血の機会を増やす必要がある。）

ケース 35 良いスピーチの方法
How to give a good speech

Track 35

⁉ スピーチの目的は、自分の意図を正しく相手に伝え、期待する行動を起こしてもらうことである。どうすれば良いスピーチになるであろうか。

ダイアローグ
Dialogue

TV anchor: The 44th **President-elect** Barack Obama **moved** people **throughout the world** with his speeches. His speeches are as **timely**, **sincere** and **persuasive** as Dr. King's speeches were. His speeches are easy to understand, so they **attract** people of every class and from every country. In Japan, his speeches are used for **improving** speaking skills. Why don't you **give it a try**?

第44代次期大統領バラクオバマはスピーチで世界中の人々を感動させました。彼のスピーチは、キング牧師のスピーチがそうだったように、時機を得ており、誠実で、説得力があります。彼のスピーチはわかりやすく、あらゆる階級やあらゆる国の人々の心を魅了します。日本では、彼のスピーチは英語のスピーキング技術を向上させるために使われています。あなたも試してみませんか。

ケース35　良いスピーチの方法

John: Hey, it's interesting that President Obama's speeches are used for improving speaking skills.

ねえ。オバマ大統領のスピーチが、英語のスピーチ技術の向上に使われているのは興味深いね。

Diana: Yeah. I'm not very good at giving speeches. So, I want to **get** good **tips on** it. Why don't we review how to give a good speech?

そうね。私はスピーチが得意じゃないの。だから、良いスピーチのコツが知りたいわ。ねえ良いスピーチをするにはどうすればいいか振り返ってみない？

John: OK. First, choose a **proper** topic, one that will **be of interest** to your **audience. Starting off** with some jokes is a good way to attract your audience.

了解。まず、聴衆が興味のある適切なトピックを選ぶんだ。ジョークで始めることが、聴衆を引き込むための良い方法の1つなんだ。

Diana: I see. Choosing a topic is very important. At the same time, knowing your audience is a **must**.

そうね。トピックの選択が、とても重要なのね。同時に聴衆を知ることが絶対必要なことね。

John: Yes. You should **be familiar with** your topic and the **content** of your speech. Then, you won't have to look at your **notes** so often.

うん。自分の選んだトピックとその内容を熟知していくべきなんだ。そうすれば、君はメモを頻繁に見る必要がない。

Diana: So you can **maintain eye contact with** your audience, right?

それすれば、聴衆とアイコンタクトをとれるのね。

John: That's right. **Conclude** your speech with a **brief summary** of your main points. **Last but not least**, success **depends on** the content of your speech. In other words, the most important thing is how well your speech is

そのとおり。最後は主要ポイントの要約でスピーチを締めくくるんだ。最後に、重要なこととして、成功はスピーチの内容次第なんだ。言い換えると、最も重要なことは君のスピーチがどれだけうまくまとまっているかだね。

179

organized.

Diana: **You've been a big help.** I'll give it a try. The best way to learn something is to do it.

すごく参考になったわ。やってみるわ。何かを学ぶのに最も良い方法は、やってみることだからね。

Words & Phrases

- □ president-elect　大統領に選出された人、次期大統領
- □ move　～の心を動かす
- □ throughout the world　世界中で
- □ timely　タイムリーな
- □ sincere　誠実な
- □ persuasive　説得力のある
- □ attract　～を魅了する
- □ improve　～を改善する
- □ give it a try　試しにやってみる
- □ get tips on ～　～のコツを得る
- □ proper　適切な
- □ be of interest　興味がある
- □ audience　聴衆、観客
- □ start off　始める
- □ must　絶対必要なもの
- □ be familiar with ～　～を熟知している
- □ content　内容
- □ note　メモ
- □ maintain eye contact with ～　～と視線を合わせる
- □ conclude　～と結論を出す
- □ brief summary　概要
- □ last but not least　最後になるが、重要なこと
- □ depend on ～　～次第である、～に頼る
- □ organize　～を整理する、～を系統立てる
- □ You've been a big help.　おかげさまで助かりました。

Tips　よく使われる表現─言い換え②─

- □ in other words
  （言い換えると）
- □ to put it simply
  （簡単に言えば）
- □ to sum up
  （要約すれば）

- [ ] in a nutshell
  (簡単に言えば)

◆その他の表現

- [ ] Why don't you give it a try?
  (試しにやってみようよ?)
- [ ] Why don't we review how to give a good speech?
  (良いスピーチのしかたを復習してみようよ。)
- [ ] the best way to learn something is to ～
  (何かを身につける一番良い方法は、～することである)

◆すぐに使える表現　Possible Opinions

- [ ] Practice makes perfect.
  (習うより慣れろ。)
- [ ] CLAP, meaning "Clearly, Loudly And with a Pause," is important.
  (CLAPが大切である。Cはハッキリと、Lは大きな声で、Pはポーズを取って話すことを意味する。)
- [ ] Put much expression into your voice.
  (声に感情を込めて話しなさい。)
- [ ] Don't talk in a monotone voice.
  (単調に話さないようにしなさい。)
- [ ] When making speeches, it's important to convey the point in a clear manner.
  (スピーチをする時、要点をハッキリ伝えることが大切である。)

ケース36 家事を平等に分担する方法
Track 36　How to share housework equally

⁉ 最近は料理男子やイクメンなど、男性の家事参加がトレンドになってきている。どうすれば家事の分担がより平等になるだろうか。

ダイアローグ
Dialogue

TV anchor: Throughout the world, men spend more time in the **workplace**. In the USA and other **developed countries**, men work an average of 5.2 hours a day and do 2.7 hours of **housework**. On the other hand, women work an average of 3.4 hours and do 4.5 hours of housework a day. Men and women spend about **the same amount of** time working every day.

世界中で、男性は職場でより多くの時間を過ごします。アメリカ合衆国やその他の先進国では、男性は一日平均5.2時間働き、家事を2.7時間しています。一方、女性は一日平均、3.4時間働き、家事を4.5時間しています。男性も女性も、毎日ほぼ同じ量の労働時間を費やしています。

ケース36　家事を平等に分担する方法

John: Wow, this is some **amazing** information. Did you know about this?

これは驚くべき情報だね。これは知っていたかい？

Diana: Yeah. I've also read about **similar** information. When **paid and unpaid working hours** are **combined**, it's found that women work longer hours than men.

ええ。似たような情報についても読んだわ。有給と無給の労働時間を合わせると、女性が男性と比べて、より長く働いていることがわかるの。

John: It's because women do almost all the housework such as cleaning, cooking and **child care**. Besides, many women work part-time. The survey said that men only **throw out** the **garbage** and clean the table **once in a while**.

それは、女性が掃除、料理や子供の世話などのすべての家事をするせいだね。しかも、多くの女性はパートで働いているからね。調査によれば、男性は時々ゴミを捨てたり、テーブルを拭いたりするだけなんだ。

Diana: What's your opinion on this information? Do you think housework can be **shared equally**?

この情報について、どう思うの？家事は平等に分担できると思う？

John: I wish I could do my share of housework, but sometimes it's difficult to do so. Men get up early to **commute to work** and come home very late.

家事の分担をしたいけど、時々難しい時もあるんだよ。男性は、通勤するのに朝早く起きて、とても遅く帰宅するんだ。

Diana: **No more excuses**! When your job ends, your time in the workplace should end. Men enjoy **going out for a drink** several times a month and enjoy their hobbies **on weekends**. But, housework never ends. When a baby

もう言い訳はいいわ。仕事が終わったら、職場での勤務時間は終わるはずでしょう。男性は月に数回、外で飲むのを楽しみ、週末に趣味を楽しんでいるわ。でも家事は決して終わらないの。赤ちゃんが泣けば、世話が必要だ

	cries, care is needed. When a room is dirty, cleaning is necessary.	わ。部屋が汚ければ、掃除が必要よ。
John:	I see your point. Housework is unpaid labor but it's work that needs to be done. Of course, I realize men can work at the office because women do housework at home.	言いたいことはわかるよ。家事は無給労働だけど、やらなければいけない仕事だよね。もちろん、女性が家事をやっているので、男性は会社で働けるのはわかるよ。
Diana:	A lot of women feel they don't **have a choice**. I feel the same. I wish I could **split** the housework **fifty-fifty**. **At the very least**, men should clean the table and cook on weekends.	多くの女性は、選択の余地がないと感じているわ。私も同じ考えよ。家事を半々にできればと思うわ。せめて、週末には、男性はテーブルを拭いて、料理すべきよね。

Words & Phrases

- workplace　職場
- developed countries　先進国
- housework　家事
- the same amount of ～　同じ量の～
- amazing　驚くほどの
- similar　同類の
- paid and unpaid working hours
  　有給と無給の労働時間
- combine　～を結合させる
- child care　育児
- throw out ～　～を捨てる

- garbage　生ゴミ、ゴミ
- once in a while　時々
- share equally　半々にする
- commute to work　通勤する
- No more excuses.　言い訳はもうたくさんです。
- go out for a drink　飲みに出かける
- on weekends　週末に
- have a choice　選ぶ権利がある
- split ～ fifty-fifty　～を半々にする
- at the very least　最低限でも

Tips よく使われる表現―出典・参照―

☐ the survey says that ～
　（調査によれば、～である）
☐ this indicates that ～
　（これは～を示している）
☐ this graph tells us that ～
　（このグラフから、～がわかる）
☐ from this, we can see that ～
　（これから、私たちには～がわかる）

◆その他の表現

☐ on the other hand
　（他方では、一方）
☐ Did you know about this?
　（これについては知っていたの？）
☐ What's your opinion on this information?
　（この情報についてはどう思うの？）
☐ I see your point.
　（言いたいことはわかる。）
☐ I feel the same.
　（私は同じ考えである。）

◆すぐに使える表現　Possible Opinions

☐ Men should exercise their right to take paternity leave.
（男性は育児休暇を取る権利を行使すべきである。）

☐ Women are expected to do all of the housework and raise their children by themselves.
（女性は一人で家事のすべてをこなし、子供を育てることを期待されている。）

☐ Women should be liberated from housework.
（女性は家事から解放されるべきである。）

☐ If men did more housework, they would not be paid overtime and the family would suffer.
（男性がもっと家事をすれば、残業手当を稼げなくなる。そして、家族が影響を受ける。）

☐ A man could become a stay-at-home dad.
（男性は、専業主夫になれる。）

ケース37 飲料水の節約方法

Track 37　How to conserve potable water

安全な飲料水の確保は人々の健康や命の問題と密接に関係する。どうすれば飲料水を節約できるだろうか。

ダイアローグ
Dialogue

TV anchor: Today, 1.5 **billion** people can't get enough potable drinking water. In 2050, it's likely that 3 to 4 billion people will **face a water shortage**. In the past, there were battles over land—now there are battles over energy. In the near future, there will be battles over water. We have to **pay** as much **attention to** water shortages as we do to air and water **pollution**.

今日、15億人の人々が、十分な飲み水を確保できていません。2050年には30億から40億の人々が水不足に直面しそうです。過去には、土地を巡る争いがありました。現在はエネルギーを巡る争いが起きています。近い将来、水を巡る争いが起こるでしょう。私たちは、大気や水質汚染に対応するのと同じように、水不足には十分な関心を払わなくてはいけません。

John: Did you know about the drinking water shortage?

飲料水不足問題について知っていたかい？

Diana: Yes, I've heard of it, but I didn't know such **data until now**. I always **take** water **for granted** because it is **obtained** so easily. I have never experienced life without enough water.

ええ、聞いたことがあるけど、今までそんなデータは知らなかったわ。私はいつも水があることを当たり前のように思っていたわ。というのも水は非常にたやすく手に入るから。私は、十分な水のない生活を経験したことがないから。

John: Neither have I. I've **been indifferent to** water usage because water is rather cheap compared to gasoline or other **necessities**.

僕もないよ。僕は水の使用に無関心だったよ。水はガソリンや他の必需品と比べて安いからさ。

Diana: But it's an **inevitable** problem we have to face.

でも、それは、私たちが直面する避けられない問題だわ。

John: Yeah, the first thing we must do is correct people's misunderstandings of water being easily **accessible** and cheap.

そうだね。私たちが最初にすべきことは、水が入手しやすく安いものだという誤解を正すことだね。

Diana: That's a good idea. Plus, we have to **take action as individuals**. I think I will **install a dishwasher**. I heard it uses 5/6 less water than washing by hand.

それは良い考えね。加えて、個人として行動に移さなくてはいけないわ。私は、食器洗い機を据え付けようと思うの。それを使うと、手で洗うよりも、水の使用量が6分の5節約できるそうなの。

John: That's a **practical measure**. Let me suggest something else. I could **pool rainwater underneath** my garden and use it for the toilet and other purposes.

それは、現実的な対策ね。僕にも一つ提案させてよ。庭の下に雨水を貯めて、それをトイレや他の用途に使いたいね。

Diana: The best way to solve this problem is for everybody to take it seriously. Then we can **make a conscientious effort** every day. There is no other way.

この問題を解決するための最善の方法は、みんなが深刻に受け止めることなの。そうすれば、毎日、ひたむきな努力を続けることができるわ。他に方法はないわ。

Words & Phrases

- billion 10億
- face a water shortage 水不足に直面する
- pay attention to ～ ～に注意を払う
- pollution 汚染
- data データ
- until now これまで
- take ～ for granted ～を当然のように考えている
- obtain ～を手に入れる
- be indifferent to ～ ～に無関心である
- necessity 必需品
- inevitable 避けられない
- accessible 入手しやすい
- take action as individuals 個人として行動を起こす
- install a dishwasher 食器洗い機を据え付ける
- practical measure 現実的な対策
- pool rainwater underneath ～ ～の下に雨水をためる
- make a conscientious effort ひたむきな努力をする

Tips よく使われる表現―提案③―

- Let me suggest something else.
  （別の提案をさせてください。）
- another opinion is to 〜
  （もうひとつの意見は〜である）
- I like your idea, but what about 〜?
  （あなたの考えは好きだけど、〜はどう？）
- I'd like to propose that 〜
  （〜を提案したい）

◆その他の表現

- did you know about 〜 issue?
  （〜の問題について知っていたの？）
- compared to 〜
  （〜と比較して）
- the first thing we must do is 〜
  （まず最初にしなければいけないことは〜である）
- That's a good idea.
  （それは良い考えである。）
- plus
  （その上）
- the best way to solve this problem is 〜
  （この問題を解決するのに最も良い方法は〜です）
- There is no other way.
  （他に方法がありません。）

ケース37　飲料水の節約方法

◆すぐに使える表現　Possible Opinions

☐ The earth is not only for humans, but for all animals and living things.
（地球は人間だけのものではなく、すべての動物や生命のためのものである。）

☐ The total amount of water used to grow vegetables, raise livestock and make machines is enormous. Thus, a water shortage may bring a food shortage as well.
（野菜を育てたり、家畜を育てたり、機械を動かしたりするのに使われる水の総量は、膨大である。そのため、水不足は、食料危機をも引き起こすかもしれない。）

☐ Developed countries should share water saving technology, such as dam construction and sewage systems, with developing countries.
（先進国は、ダムの建設、下水道システムのような水を節約する技術を、発展途上国と共有すべきである。）

☐ In preparation for a water shortage, we need to invent machines that purify salt water on a large scale.
（水不足に備えて、大規模に塩水を浄化させる機械を発明する必要がある。）

ケース 38 英語力を身につける方法
Track 38　How to acquire English language skills

⁉ グローバル化が進めば進むほど、英語の必要性は大きくなる傾向にある。どうすれば効果的に英語を身につけられるだろうか。

ダイアローグ
Dialogue

TV anchor: It's **truly** a **pity** to see that many Japanese people **are unable to** communicate in English despite the fact that they have studied it for more than 10 years, from elementary school to college. It's clear that English is the **global** language. Without **a good command of English**, Japanese people will not be able to **play important roles in** the business world.

多くの日本人が小学校から大学まで、10年間以上も英語を勉強している事実にもかかわらず、英語でコミュニケーションをとることができないことは、本当に残念です。英語は国際語であることは明らかです。英語を自由に使いこなすことができなくては、日本人がビジネス界で重要な役割を担うことができなくなるでしょう。

ケース38 英語力を身につける方法

John: Why do you think Japanese people can't communicate in English?

どうして日本人は英語でコミュニケーションをとることができないと思う？

Diana: Well, there are problems with **authorized textbooks**, the quality of English teachers, the **lack of opportunities** to speak English in Japan…, there are tons of reasons. It seems to me that Japanese don't have clear goals in studying English. The most important point for Japanese is to have clear goals.

そうね。検定教科書の問題、英語教師の質、日本国内で英語を話す機会の不足など、数え切れないほど理由はあるわ。日本人は英語の学習に明確な目標を持っていないように思えるわ。日本人にとって最も重要な点は明確な目標を持つことね。

John: What are you implying?

何が言いたいの？

Diana: One famous English specialist **suggests** the S-M-A-R-T-S **approach** to set up goals for English study. S means "**Specific**," **that is**, it's important to have specific and clear goals in English study. M stands for "**Measurable**." It's important to check your level of English with TOEIC or STEP tests in order to improve your English skills. A stands for "**Attainable**" goals.

ある有名な英語の専門家が、英語学習に目標を設定するためのSMARTS学習法を提案しているわ。Sは「明確な」を意味するの。つまり、英語学習には、明確な目標を持つことが大切なの。Mは「測定可能な」を意味するの。英語力を向上させるためには、TOEICや英語検定試験などで英語力を測定することが大切なの。Aは「達成できる」目標を意味するわ。

John: I see. What do R and T stand for?

なるほど。RとTは何を意味するの？

Diana: R stands for "Realistic." Goals should be **realistic** to continue studying. T stands for "**Time-bound**." **Deadlines** to **accomplish goals** should be set up. The last…

Rは「現実的な」を意味するわ。目標は学習し続けるために現実的であるべきなの。Tは「期限を決めた」を意味するわ。目標を達成するための期限を設定する必要があるの。最後の…

193

John: Let me **give it a try**. It must be "**Sacrifice**" of time.

僕に当てさせて。Ｓは時間の「犠牲」に違いないね。

Diana: Good try. You are **partially correct**. You **are required to** sacrifice a lot of time as well as lots of money to have a good command of English.

やるじゃない。部分的には正解ね。英語を自由に使いこなすことができるようにするには、たくさんのお金とたくさんの時間を犠牲にする必要があるわ。

Words & Phrases

- ☐ truly　全く
- ☐ pity　残念なこと
- ☐ be unable to ～　～することができない
- ☐ global　グローバルな
- ☐ have a good command of English　英語が堪能である
- ☐ play an important role in ～　～に重要な役割を果たす
- ☐ authorized textbook　検定教科書
- ☐ lack of opportunity　チャンスの少なさ
- ☐ suggest　～を提案する
- ☐ approach　学習法
- ☐ specific　具体的な
- ☐ that is (to say)　すなわち
- ☐ measurable　測定可能な
- ☐ attainable　達成できる
- ☐ realistic　現実的な
- ☐ time-bound　期限を決めた
- ☐ deadline　期限
- ☐ accomplish one's goal　目標を達成する
- ☐ give it a try　試してみる
- ☐ sacrifice　犠牲、～を犠牲にする
- ☐ partially correct　部分的に正しい
- ☐ be required to ～　～するよう義務づけられている

ケース38　英語力を身につける方法

Tips よく使われる表現―確認④―

- What are you implying?
  （何が言いたいのですか。）
- What do you intend to do?
  （何をするつもりですか）
- what do you mean by 〜?
  （〜はどういう意味ですか）
- what does it mean by 〜?
  （〜はどういう意味ですか）

◆その他の表現

- despite the fact that 〜
  （〜という事実にもかかわらず）
- there are tons of reasons for 〜
  （〜にはたくさんの理由がある）
- the most important point is to 〜
  （一番重要なことは〜することである）
- What do R and T stand for?
  （RとTはどういう意味なの？）

◆すぐに使える表現　Possible Opinions

- It's important to enjoy studying English, not to endure it.
  （英語学習は耐えるのではなく、楽しむことが大切である。）
- Try to remember and use English phrases you find interesting and effective.
  （あなたが興味深く効果的だと思う英語のフレーズを覚えて、使おうとしなさい。）

☐ It's necessary to actively use English words and phrases after you've learned them.
（英語の単語やフレーズを学習した後に、それらを積極的に活用することが必要である。）

☐ Learners should be given chances to express their own ideas in English.
（学習者は英語で自分の考えを表現するチャンスを与えられるべきである。）

ケース39 食品廃棄物を減らす方法
Track 39   How to decrease food waste

⁉ 本来食べられる食品が年間を通して大量に廃棄されている。どうすれば食品廃棄物を減らすことができるのだろうか。

ダイアローグ
Dialogue

TV anchor: According to an **alarming** report, about 30 to 50 percent of all the food **produced** in the world is **wasted**. On the other hand, it is said that one out of eight people in poor countries is **malnourished**.

驚くべき報告によると、世界で生産される食品の約30%〜50%が廃棄されています。一方、貧しい国々では、8人に1人が栄養失調だと言われています。

John: I didn't know food waste was this big of a problem. Are there any special reasons why we have so much food waste?

僕は食品廃棄物がこれほど大きな問題だと知らなかったよ。これほど多くの食品廃棄物がある何か特別な理由があるのかい?

Diana:	Yeah, there are two reasons. First, people in **advanced countries tend to** cook more food than they can eat and **throw away** the **uneaten food**. Second, we tend to worry about the **sell-by date** too much.	ええ、2つの理由があるわ。1つ目は、先進国の人々は自分たちが食べることができる以上の量の食品を調理して、食べ残した食品を廃棄する傾向にあるの。2つ目は、私たちは、販売期限をあまりにも気にする傾向にあるわ。
John:	I see. So what should we do then to **reduce food waste**?	なるほど。それで食品廃棄物を減らすには何をしたらいいの？
Diana:	Well, we should buy **smaller amounts of** food and eat what we have in our **fridges** first. Then we won't have to waste food so much. Sometimes we should not worry too much about the sell-by date because the sell-by date is not **the same as** the **use-by date**.	そうね。より少量の食品を買って、まず、冷蔵庫の中に残っているものから食べるべきね。そうすれば私たちはそれほど食品を廃棄しなくてもよくなるわ。私たちは販売期限を心配し過ぎるべきでないわ。販売期限は消費期限とは異なるので。
John:	That's a point I didn't notice, but do you mean even a few days after the sell-by date, food is still **edible**?	その点には僕は気づかなかったよ。でも、販売期限を数日過ぎても、食品はまだ食べられるってことだよね？
Diana:	That's right. It just becomes less **tasty** than before. Actually, the taste of food a few days after the sell-by date tastes almost the same. You can buy it cheaper then too.	そのとおりよ。少し味が落ちるだけよ。実際に、食品の味は、販売期限を過ぎた数日後でも、ほとんど同じなのよ。値段も安くなるわ。
John:	Oh, I see. **Thanks for the tip.**	なるほど。良い情報をありがとう。

Words & Phrases

- alarming　驚くべき、警戒すべき
- produce　〜を生産する
- waste　〜を無駄にする
- malnourished　栄養失調の
- advanced countries　先進国
- tend to 〜　〜する傾向がある
- throw away 〜　〜を投げ捨てる
- uneaten food　食べ残し
- sell-by date　販売期限（通常、消費期限より少し前）
- reduce　〜を減らす
- food waste　食品廃棄物
- a small amount of 〜　少量の〜
- fridge　冷蔵庫
- the same as 〜　〜と同じ
- use-by date　消費期限
- edible　食べられる
- tasty　おいしい
- Thanks for the tip.　良い情報をくれてありがとう。

Tips　よく使われる表現—理由②—

- are there any special reasons why 〜 ?
  （〜だという特別な理由があるの？）
- do you know why 〜 ?
  （あなたはなぜ〜か知っている？）
- why do you think 〜 ?
  （どうして〜だと思うの？）
- are there good reasons why 〜 ?
  （〜 だという正当な理由はあるの？）

◆その他の表現

- according to an alarming report
  （驚くべき報告書によると）
- on the other hand
  （一方）
- there are two reasons
  （2つの理由がある）

☐ that's a point I didn't notice, but ～
(それは私が気づかなかった点であるが、～)

◆すぐに使える表現　Possible Opinions

☐ People must pay more attention to shopping and eating habits. It is not unlikely that people in developed countries throw away as much as half the food they buy.
(人々は、買い物や食生活には、より注意を払わなければならない。たぶん、先進国の人々は、購入した食品の半分は廃棄している。)

☐ We need to educate citizens to reduce food waste.
(私たちは、食品のムダを削減するために市民を教育する必要がある。)

☐ In Tokyo alone, people waste about 6,000 tons of food daily, which is enough to keep 4.5 million starving people alive for a day.
(東京だけでも、人々は毎日約6000トンの食品を廃棄している。その量は450万人の飢えた人々が1日生きながらえるに十分な量である。)

☐ We should start providing doggy bags. It's natural for us to take home the leftovers from our meals.
(私たちはドギーバッグを提供し始めるべきである。食事の食べ残しを家に持ち帰ることは、自然なことである。)

ケース 40　退職する？　働き続ける？

Track 40　Retire or keep working, if you won the lottery?

宝くじに当選した人は、退職するのか働き続けるのか。どちらが良いだろうか。

ダイアローグ
Dialogue

TV anchor: Last week, a man **was arrested for** killing his girlfriend just after she won 300 million yen in the **lottery**. In the end the woman was not as lucky as she thought.

先週、一人の男性が交際相手を殺した罪で逮捕されました。交際相手は宝くじで3億円を当てた直後でした。結局、その女性は、思った程幸運ではありませんでした。

John: What a sad story, huh?

なんて切ない話なんだ。

Diana: Yeah! Money can really change a person's life. Would you **quit** your job if you won 300 million yen in the lottery?

そうね。お金が本当に人の人生を変えてしまうのね。もし宝くじで3億円当てたら、仕事は辞めるの？

John: Me? Of course I wouldn't. I would still work if I won the lottery. I love my job. This job is what makes my life **worth** living.

僕が？もちろん、辞めないよ。もし宝くじに当たっても働き続けるよ。仕事を愛しているし。この仕事は自分の人生の生きがいなんだ。

Diana: I think it would probably be difficult to **continue** working at your job. Imagine what would happen to you if your friends knew that you had become a **millionaire**? Money **creates envy**. It would become very difficult for you to **get along with** your friends.

おそらく仕事で働き続けるのは難しいと思うわ。もし友達が、あなたが億万長者になったと知ればどうなるか考えてみてよ。お金はねたみを作るわ。友達と仲良くするのが難しくなるわ。

John: If my friends changed their **attitudes toward** me because of money, I would know they aren't real friends. Besides, I'm sure my friends would not change their attitudes. What about you?

もし僕の友達が、お金が理由で態度を変えるのなら、彼らが、本当の友達でないと気づくだけさ。それに僕の友達はきっと態度を変えないよ。君はどうなの？

Diana: I would not let my friends know of my good fortune. I would give up my job and house, and leave my friends behind within a month. Then, I wouldn't have to worry about keeping my wealth secret from others. I would start a new life somewhere and **make the most of** that new life with the prize money. For example, I'd buy a **Mercedes convertible** and take a long vacation in Dubai.

私は友達には自分の幸運について知らせないわ。私は仕事も家も諦めて、1カ月以内に友達から離れるわ。そうすれば、自分のお金の秘密を内緒にしておく心配をしなくてもすむわ。どこかで新しい人生を始めて、賞金で新しい人生を思いっきり楽しむわ。例えば、メルセデスのオープンカーを買ったり、ドバイで長期休暇をとったりするわ。

John: I doubt your idea would work. I'd just want

君の考えがうまくいくとは思わない。僕はお金よ

ケース40　退職する？　働き続ける？

　　　　　　to put my friends before money. | り友達を大切にしたいんだ。

Diana: People quickly change their attitudes when money is **involved**. **You'll see.** | お金が絡むと、人々は態度をすぐに変えるわ。今にわかるわ。

Words & Phrases

- be arrested for ~　～で逮捕される
- lottery　宝くじ
- quit　～をやめる
- worth　～の価値がある
- continue　～し続ける
- millionaire　大金持ち
- create　～を作る
- envy　ねたみ
- get along with ~　～と仲良くする
- attitude　態度
- toward　～に対する
- make the most of ~　～を最大限活用する
- Mercedes convertible　オープンカーのメルセデス
- involve　～を伴う
- You'll see.　今に分かるさ。

Tips よく使われる表現―疑問―

☐ I doubt your idea would work.
　（あなたの考えがうまくいくか疑問を抱いている。）
☐ I have my doubts about what you've just said.
　（私はあなたが今言ったことについて疑念を持っている。）
☐ I don't think your idea will work.
　（あなたのアイディアがうまくいくとは思わない。）
☐ I have doubts about your opinion.
　（あなたの意見には疑問を抱いている。）

◆その他の表現

☐ in the end
　（ついに）
☐ besides
　（その上）
☐ What about you?
　（あなたはどうなの？）
☐ for example
　（例えば）

◆すぐに使える表現　Possible Opinions

- ☐ I would start my own business.
  （自分で事業を始める。）
- ☐ I would do something good for others, such as donating money to charity.
  （僕は例えば、お金をチャリティーに寄付するなど、他の人のために何かをする。）
- ☐ I would get a more relaxed job.
  （僕はもっとのんびりとした仕事に就く。）
- ☐ I would quit my job and go to law school.
  （仕事を辞めて、法科大学院に進む。）
- ☐ I will invest the prize money I won in the stock market. I want to profit from trading stocks.
  （儲けた賞金を株式市場に投資するだろう。私は、株売買で儲けたい。）

ケース41　新聞？　インターネット？

Track 41

Newspapers or the Internet?

新聞とインターネットの情報には、それぞれメリットとデメリットがある。どちらが情報収集するには良いのだろうか。

ダイアローグ
Dialogue

TV anchor: To **increase viewer ratings**, the **mass media invades** people's **private lives** too much. They **conduct interviews** without considering people's right to privacy. They interview **victims** of **crimes** and accidents, and even their family members **aggressively**. It's time to think about the media's **careless actions**.

視聴率を上げるために、マスコミは人々の私生活をあまりにも侵害しています。マスコミは、人々のプライバシーの権利を考慮せずにインタビューします。犯罪や事故の被害者や家族にでさえ攻撃的にインタビューします。マスコミの不注意な行動について一考する時期なのではないでしょうか。

John: I hate the mass media's **arrogant attitude**.

僕は、マスコミの横柄な態度が嫌いだね。

ケース41 新聞？ インターネット？

Diana: Yeah, reporters like the **paparazzi** do anything to **enhance the news value** of a story.

パパラッチのような、レポーターは、報道価値を高めるために、何でもするからね。

John: Famous people are often **harassed** by them. By the way, how do you prefer to get your news, newspapers or the Internet?

有名人は、しばしば彼らに悩まされているよ。ところで、ニュースは新聞とインターネットのどちらから入手する方がいい？

Diana: I rely on newspapers for information, opinions and **perspective**. They are easy to read.

私は情報、意見、大局観については新聞を頼りにしているわ。新聞の方が読み取りやすいわ。

John: I think the Internet is the most convenient, because it's easy to **obtain** information quickly.

僕はインターネットが最も便利だね。というのも情報が速く入手しやすいからね。

Diana: The reason why I like newspapers is their **reliability**. I admit the Internet is quick and convenient for finding certain information. But, much of the information on the Internet may be **inadequate** or inaccurate. Inaccurate information is sure to **have a harmful influence on** society.

私が新聞を好きな理由は、信頼性なの。インターネットは、特定の情報を見つけるのに速くて、便利よ。でも、インターネット上の多くの情報は不適切か不正確かもしれないわ。不正確な情報は、必ず社会に悪影響を及ぼすわ。

John: **In a sense**, you're right about its reliability. However, I am **cautious** not to **take** the news **at face value**. Even with newspapers, there are two types: **right-leaning** and **left-leaning**. Sometimes newspaper editors **omit** or **censor** articles that are unfavorable to their opinions. They are sometimes **biased** to attract readers' attention. In the case of the Internet, however,

情報の信頼性については、ある意味、君は正しいよ。でも、僕は、警戒して報道を額面どおりに受け取らないんだ。新聞でさえ、右寄りや左寄りの2つのタイプがあるよね。時々、新聞の編集者は自分たちの意見に好ましくない記事は、一部省略したり、検閲したりするんだ。時には読者の注意を引きつけるために報道が偏るんだ。でも、インターネットの場合に

I can **search for** the **articles** and **cross-reference** them immediately. There is no other form of media that can provide such a large amount of information so quickly. | は、自分で記事を検索し、それらをすぐに相互参照できるんだ。それ程多くの情報量をそれ程素早く提供してくれるメディア媒体は他にないのさ。

Diana: I still prefer newspapers for their **in-depth coverage** of the news. | 私は、それでも詳しいニュース記事を提供してくれる新聞が好きだわ。

Words & Phrases

- increase viewer ratings　視聴率を上げる
- mass media　マスコミ
- invade a private life　私生活を侵害する
- conduct an interview　インタビューを行う
- consider　よく考える
- victim　被害者
- crime　犯罪
- aggressively　積極的に
- careless action　軽率な行動
- arrogant attitude　横柄な態度
- paparazzi　パパラッチ
- enhance the news value　報道価値を高める
- harass　〜を悩ませる
- perspective　考え方、大局観
- obtain　〜を得る
- reliability　信頼性
- inadequate　不適切な
- inaccurate　不正確な
- have a harmful influence on 〜　〜に悪い影響を及ぼす
- in a sense　ある意味で
- cautious　用心深い
- take 〜 at face value　〜を額面どおりに受け止める
- right-leaning　右寄りの
- left-leaning　左寄りの
- omit　〜を除く
- censor　〜を検閲する
- biased　偏見を抱いた
- search for 〜　〜を探す
- article　記事
- cross-reference　〜を相互参照する
- in-depth coverage　踏みこんだ深い記事

Tips よく使われる表現 ―理由③―

- [ ] let me explain why ~
  (~である理由を説明する)
- [ ] the reason is that ~
  (その理由は~である)
- [ ] Let me show you 3 reasons why I am against the plan. First ~. Second…
  (その計画に反対する理由を3つ説明する。第1は~、第2は….)
- [ ] I have 3 reasons why I think so.
  (そう思う3つの理由がある。)

◆その他の表現

- [ ] by the way
  (ところで)
- [ ] how do you prefer to get ~ ?
  (どのように~を入手するのが好きなの?)
- [ ] because it's easy to ~
  (というのは~することが簡単だからである)
- [ ] however
  (しかしながら)
- [ ] in the case of the Internet
  (インターネットの場合には)

◆すぐに使える表現　Possible Opinions

- [ ] It's necessary to ban misleading information on the Internet.
  （インターネット上の誤解を与える情報を禁止することは必要である。）
- [ ] It's necessary to find out what information is correct and trustworthy out of the tremendous amount of information we get on the Internet.
  （インターネット上で私たちが得る膨大な量の情報から、どの情報が正しくて、信頼できるか見破ることが必要である。）
- [ ] The Internet cannot provide us with a profound insight of the news.
  （インターネットは、深い洞察のあるニュースは提供してくれない。）
- [ ] People need to obtain precise data, evidence and information to understand the news.
  （人々は、ニュースを理解するために、正確なデータ、証拠、情報を入手する必要がある。）
- [ ] I need to learn how to utilize the information I get on the Internet.
  （インターネットで収集した情報の活用方法を身につける必要がある。）

ケース 42 米？ パン？

Track 42 — Rice or bread?

食生活の変化により、米の消費量が年々減っている。米とパン、食事ではどちらが好まれるのだろうか。

ダイアローグ
Dialogue

TV anchor: In Japan, **per capita** rice **consumption** is **decreasing** while per capita **bread** consumption is increasing. Japan's food **self-sufficiency rate** was 39% this year. Despite this fact, rice production has **exceeded** consumption **for the past two decades**.

日本では、パンの一人当たりの消費量が増えている一方、米の一人当たりの消費量が減少しています。日本の今年の食料自給率は39%でした。この事実にもかかわらず、過去20年間、米の生産は消費を上回っています。

John: Which do you like better, rice or bread?

お米とパンでは、どっちが好きかな？

Diana: I like rice better because it's tastier and healthier than bread. Rice is **digested** slowly, so I feel full for a long time. On the other hand, I feel hungry soon after I eat bread. How about you?

私は、パンより美味しくて健康的だから、お米が好きだわ。お米は、腹持ちがよいので、長時間満腹感が得られるの。一方、パンを食べた後すぐ、お腹が空いてしまうの。あなたはどうなの？

John: I like bread better because there is a large variety of bread such as **croissants**, banana bread and **raisin** bread.

僕は、パンが好きだね。クロワッサン、バナナブレッド、レーズンブレッドのように、非常にたくさんの種類のパンがあるからね。

Diana: That may be true, but there are also many ways to cook rice. For example, rice cakes, **stir-fried rice** and rice cooked with **chestnuts** are all rice-based dishes. Rice is a low-calorie food and sake is even made from good quality rice.

そうかもしれないけど、お米を調理する方法だってたくさんあるわ。例えば、お餅、チャーハン、栗ご飯は、全部、お米の料理よ。お米は、低カロリーだし、お酒も上質のお米から作られるのよ。

John: You're right. By the way, did you know that bread made of rice **flour** is getting popular?

そうだね。ところで、米粉からできたパンが人気だって知っているかい？

Diana: No, I didn't. **What's it like?**

いいえ、知らないわ。どんな感じのなの？

John: It's moist and has a **sweet rice flavor**. I like to eat it with blueberry jam.

しっとりとして、甘いお米の風味だね。ブルーベリージャムで食べるのが好きなんだ。

Diana: Can you eat rice with jam? Is it **bread-shaped rice** or **rice-flavored bread**? I'd like to taste it someday, but today let's agree to disagree.

お米をジャムで食べることができるの？パンの形をしたお米なの、それともお米風味のパンなの？いつか食べてみたいわ。でも、今日は反対することに同意するわ。

ケース42 米？ パン？

Words & Phrases

- per capita　一人当たりの
- consumption　消費量
- decrease　減る
- self-sufficiency rate　自給率
- exceed　〜を超える
- for the past two decades　過去20年間で
- digest　〜を消化する
- croissant　クロワッサン
- raisin　レーズン
- stir-fried rice　チャーハン
- chestnut　クリ
- flour　小麦粉
- What's it like?　それはどんな感じですか。
- sweet rice flavor　甘い米の香り
- bread-shaped rice　パンの形をした米
- rice-flavored bread　米の風味のするパン

Tips　よく使われる表現─逆接②─

- despite 〜
  （〜にもかかわらず）
- in spite of 〜
  （〜にもかかわらず）
- nevertheless
  （それにもかかわらず）
- regardless of 〜
  （〜にもかかわらず）

◆その他の表現

- **Which do you like better, rice or bread?**
  （お米とパンどちらが好きなの？）
- **I like rice better because 〜**
  （〜という理由でお米が好きです。）
- **on the other hand**
  （一方）

213

- ☐ How about you?
  （あなたはどうなの？）
- ☐ that may be true, but ~
  （それは真実かもしれないが、～）
- ☐ for example
  （例えば）
- ☐ by the way
  （ところで）
- ☐ Let's agree to disagree.
  （同意しないことに同意しよう。）

◆すぐに使える表現　Possible Opinions

- ☐ Freshly baked bread is delicious.
  （焼きたてのパンは美味しい。）
- ☐ Bread can be a high calorie food with jam and butter.
  （パンはジャムとバターで、高カロリーになり得る。）
- ☐ Rice doesn't go bad.
  （米は悪くならない。）
- ☐ Freshly cooked rice tastes delicious.
  （炊きたてのお米は美味しい。）
- ☐ People have different tastes in food.
  （人は食べ物の好みが違う。）

ケース43 弁当？ 給食？

Track 43

Boxed lunch or school lunch?

弁当と給食、親の立場や子供の立場によって意見が違う。昼食はどちらが好まれるのだろうか。

ダイアローグ
Dialogue

TV anchor: Elementary and junior high school **attendance** is **compulsory** in Japan, so parents don't have to **pay tuition** for public schools. School lunches are **provided at a reasonable price** in most public elementary and junior high schools. But, some parents don't want to pay lunch **fees**. Therefore, **the amount of** unpaid school lunch fees is increasing every year. It's a big problem now.

日本では、小学校と中学校の就学は、義務教育です。そのため、保護者は公立学校の授業料は払う必要がありません。ほとんどの小学校と中学校で学校給食が、お手頃価格で提供されます。しかし、保護者の中には給食費を払いたくない人もいます。そのため、給食費未納の総額が毎年増えています。今や大問題です。

John:	I liked the curried rice and **mango pudding** served in school lunch.	僕は学校給食で出されるカレーピラフとマンゴープリンが好きだったな。
Diana:	Really? I **had no choice but** a boxed lunch, but I liked boxed lunches better. I felt excited every time I opened my boxed lunch because I was always pleasantly surprised by the food in it. Also, my mom didn't put any food I didn't like in my lunch.	そうなの？私には弁当しか選択肢がなかったけど、私は弁当が好きだったわ。私は弁当の中のおかずにいつもうれしい驚きがあったので、弁当を開ける度にワクワクしたわ。また、母が私の嫌いなおかずは弁当に入れなかったの。
John:	Didn't you worry about your mom? She **used to** get up early, think about what to make, and make it for you every day. I'm sure **it was** quite **a bother**.	お母さんの心配はしなかったの？彼女は早く起きて、何を作るか考えて、弁当を毎日作っていたんだろう。弁当作りは面倒だったと思うよ。
Diana:	No, I don't think so. She likes cooking.	いいえ、そう思わないわ。母は、料理が好きなのよ。
John:	Even so, the fact is that she woke up very early every morning. If you had eaten school lunch, she wouldn't have had to get up so early. Besides, school lunch is a **well-balanced meal** planned by **nutritionists**.	それでも、実際、彼女は毎朝かなり早く起きていたんだよ。もし君が学校給食を食べていたら、彼女はそんなに早く起きる必要はなかったんだよ。それに、学校給食は管理栄養士に計画されたバランスの良い食事なんだよ。
Diana:	A well-balanced meal does not mean **delicious** food. So you sometimes had to eat foods you disliked. Right?	バランスの良い食事は美味しい食べ物とは限らないわ。だから、時々嫌いな食べ物を食べなくてはならなかったでしょう。そうでしょう？
John:	That's true, but everything we ate was good for us. Above all, I **fondly remember** eating	それは事実だけど、すべて私たちにとって栄養があるんだ。結局、僕は、懐かしく毎日学校給食を

school lunch with my classmates every day.	クラスメートと食べていたことを思い出すよ。
Diana: Well, I enjoyed eating different food at school. I also have good memories of eating lunch at school. It's not a matter of lunch style, but a matter of the fun we had together during lunch.	私は、学校でいろいろな食べ物を食べて楽しかったわ。私も学校で昼食を食べたことは良い思い出ね。昼食のスタイルの問題ではなく、一緒に昼食を食べて楽しかったかってことよね。

Words & Phrases

- attendance 出席、就学
- compulsory 義務の
- pay tuition 授業料を払う
- provide ～を供給する
- at a reasonable price 手頃な価格で
- fee 料金
- the amount of ～ ～の総計
- mango pudding マンゴープリン
- have no choice but ～ ～する他に選択の余地がない

- used to ～ よく～していたものだ
- It's a bother. 面倒くさい。
- well-balanced meal よくバランスのとれた食事
- nutritionist 栄養士
- delicious おいしい
- fondly remember 懐かしく思い出す

Tips　よく使われる表現―追加―

- [ ] besides
    （さらに）
- [ ] moreover
    （さらに）
- [ ] furthermore
    （さらに）
- [ ] in addition to that 〜
    （〜に加えて）
- [ ] on top of that 〜
    （〜に加えて）
- [ ] what is more
    （さらに）
- [ ] plus
    （さらに）

◆その他の表現

- [ ] therefore
    （それゆえに）
- [ ] I like 〜 better
    （〜がより好きである）
- [ ] No, I don't think so.
    （いいえ、私はそう思わない。）
- [ ] the fact is that 〜
    （実は〜である）
- [ ] above all
    （中でも）
- [ ] It's not a matter of 〜 , but a matter of …
    （〜の問題ではなく、…の問題である）

ケース43　弁当？　給食？

> ◆すぐに使える表現　Possible Opinions

- ☐ School lunches are more convenient and better for your health.
  （学校給食はより便利で、健康にとって良い。）
- ☐ You have to eat a lot of vegetables or fish even if you don't like them.
  （たとえ好きでなくても、たくさんの野菜や魚を食べなくてはならない。）
- ☐ I can bring as much food as I want in a boxed lunch.
  （弁当なら、自分が欲しい分量をもってくることができる。）
- ☐ Checking allergy-causing ingredients for students with food allergies is bothersome.
  （食物アレルギーのある生徒にとってアレルギーを誘発する原料を調べることは、煩わしい。）

ケース44　愛？　お金？
Track 44　Love or money?

幸せに関する意識調査では、世帯年収が上がっても、幸福度の上昇率の差は小さくなる。結婚にはどちらがより必要なのだろうか。

ダイアローグ
Dialogue

TV anchor: Many people **argue over the topic**, "Which is more important, love or money?" There are many merits to both, but **ultimately**, in today's world, money seems to be the most important thing in our lives. Simply look at the many people who **become absorbed in** the stock market.

愛とお金、どっちが大切かというトピックに関して、多くの人が議論します。両方には多くのメリットがあります。しかし、究極的には、今日の世界では、人生の中でお金が最も大切なように思われます。株取引に熱中する多くの人々を見てください。

Diana: I don't think so. The most important thing is

私はそう思わないわ。最

ケース44 愛？ お金？

love. Love is a natural thing; money is not.

も大切なものは愛だわ。愛は自然なもので、お金は違うわ。

John: I disagree with you. Plus, what you're saying is too abstract. Give me some examples.

僕は君に賛成しないよ。しかも君の言っていることは、抽象的過ぎだよ。いくつか具体例を示してよ。

Diana: For example, you can buy a house with money, but can you buy a home **filled with** love?

例えば、お金で家は買えるけど、愛で満たされた家庭は買えないわ。

John: Well…. As human beings, all we need to live is **food, clothing and shelter**. These **necessities** are not free, so we need money to buy them.

そうだね。人間として、生きるために必要なものは、衣食住だよ。これらの必需品は無料じゃない。だから買うためのお金が必要なんだ。

Diana: You can buy **medicine** with money, but not health. Don't you think people need love, too?

お金で薬は買えるけど、健康は買えないわ。人々には愛も必要だと思わない？

John: You're right. But even that costs money. Women like it when I buy them nice things. So, I need money to go out with my girlfriend.

思うよ。でも、愛にもお金がかかるんだ。女性は素敵なものを買ってあげると喜ぶんだ。だから、彼女と付き合うのにお金が必要なんだ。

Diana: I don't think so. The only nice thing your girlfriend wants is true love. Besides, when we die, we can't take anything with us. I'm sure love stays with us **forever**, even after we die.

私は、そうは思わないわ。あなたの彼女が欲しい唯一のものは、本当の愛よ。それに、死んだ時には、私たちは何も持って行くことはできないわ。死んだ後でも、愛は、きっと永遠に私たちと共に残るのよ。

John: I know money can't buy happiness. I also know it's possible to **fall in love with** a poor

お金で幸せを買うことができないことはわかるさ。一目惚れで貧しい人に恋に落ちることもある

person **at first sight**, but I'm sure it's difficult to live a happy life without **a certain amount of** money.

と思うよ。でも、きっとある程度のお金がなくては、幸福な人生を送ることは難しいよ。

Words & Phrases

- argue over the topic　トピックについて論じる
- ultimately　最終的に
- become absorbed in 〜　〜に夢中になる
- stock market　株取引、株式市場
- be filled with 〜　〜で満たされる
- food, clothing and shelter　衣食住
- necessities　必需品
- medicine　薬
- forever　永遠に
- fall in love with 〜　〜と恋に落ちる
- at first sight　一目で
- a certain amount of 〜　ある一定量の〜

ケース44 愛？ お金？

Tips よく使われる表現—不明確さの指摘—

- What you're saying is too abstract. Give me some examples.
  （あなたが言っていることは、あまりにも抽象的である。いくつか例を示してください。）
- That's a broad statement. Could you be more specific?
  （それは、大まかな発言だね。もっと具体的に言ってくれますか。）
- Your opinion is vague. Give me some examples.
  （あなたの意見は曖昧である。いくつか例を示してください。）
- Your idea is illogical.
  （あなたの考えは非論理的である。）

◆ その他の表現

- Which is more important, love or money?
  （愛とお金のどちらが大切ですか。）
- there are many merits to both, but ～
  （両方に多くのメリットはあるが～）
- the most important thing is ～
  （最も大切なものは～である）
- I disagree with you.
  （あなたに反対である。）
- plus
  （その上）
- for example
  （例えば）
- I don't think so.
  （私はそうは思わない。）
- besides
  （さらに）

- ☐ all we need to live is 〜

    (生きる上で必要なことは〜である)

◆すぐに使える表現　Possible Opinions

- ☐ Everyone needs money. You can't eat or handle all family finances without it.

    (みんなお金を必要とする。お金なしでは、食べていくことも家計のすべてをやりくりすることもできない。)
- ☐ Being together is more important than all that fancy stuff.

    (一緒にいることが、すべての高級なものよりも大切である。)
- ☐ Good chemistry between two people is more important than money.

    (2人の間の密接な関係がお金より大切である。)
- ☐ Money talks.

    (金がものを言う。)
- ☐ Love is what matters.

    (愛が大切である。)
- ☐ Some people may get married to rich people out of greed.

    (金銭欲のために金持ちと結婚する人がいるかもしれない。)

ケース45 制服？ 私服？

Track 45

School uniforms or ordinary clothes?

個性の時代やオンリーワンの時代といわれながら、制服の高校が多い。制服と私服のどちらがより好まれるのだろうか。

ダイアローグ
Dialogue

TV anchor: Some high schools in Tokyo don't have **school uniforms**. It's becoming popular among the students of such high schools to wear the uniforms of another school **possibly** because they enjoy wearing school uniforms or they don't want to **choose** their own clothes every morning.

制服のない高校が東京にいくつかあります。そんな高校の生徒の間で、他の学校の制服を着ることが流行しています。制服を着ることを楽しんでいるのかもしれませんし、毎朝私服を選ぶ手間をかけたくないからかもしれません。

John: Would you want to wear a school uniform?

制服を着てみたいと思う？

Diana: Yeah, it's good because choosing my clothes every morning is **tiring**. It's **time-consuming**, too.

ええ。制服は良いわ。毎朝、私服を選ぶのは面倒だわ。時間もかかるしね。

John: I don't think so. Choosing my clothes every morning is fun. In addition, I can **express my individuality through my clothes**.

僕はそう思わないよ。毎朝、私服を選ぶのは、楽しいよ。それに、私服をとおして個性を表現できるよね。

Diana: Do you mean you like to choose your clothes every day?

毎日、私服を選ぶのが、好きってことなの？

John: Why not? I enjoy choosing clothes to wear every morning. I can **relax** and **concentrate on** my work better when I wear the clothes I like.

どうして好きじゃないの？毎朝、私服を選ぶのは楽しいよ。自分のお気に入りの服を着ると、よりリラックスして、仕事に集中できるよ。

Diana: If I don't wear a school uniform, I'll have to **purchase** clothes to wear both inside and outside of school. It's a waste of money to buy extra clothes. School uniforms are more **reasonably priced** than ordinary clothes. Plus, wearing the same school uniform **provides a sense of unity** among students.

もし、制服を着なければ、私は学校の中外で着る服を買わなければいけないわ。着替えを買うのはお金のムダでしょう。学校の制服は、普段着よりも手ごろな価格だわ。それに、同じ学校の制服を着ることは、生徒に一体感をもたらしてくれるわ。

John: Are you absolutely sure of that? In schools, students **share** space, time, events and classes. I'm sure they feel a sense of unity by experiencing **various aspects of school life** together. They don't have to wear the same

それを本気で言っているのかい？学校では生徒は空間、時間、行事や授業を共有するんだよ。彼らは、学校生活の様々なことを一緒に経験することで、きっと一体感を味わっているよ。一体感を味わうのに学校で制服を着る必要はないよ。

ケース45 制服？ 私服？

uniforms at school to feel that.

Diana: Perhaps you're right, but by wearing the same school uniform, it's easier to feel a sense of unity as a school. Besides, I like the **design** of my school uniform.

> たぶんそうかもしれないわ、でも同じ制服を着ることで、学校としての一体感を味わいやすいのよ。しかも、私は自分の学校の制服のデザインが気に入っているわ。

Words & Phrases

- school uniform 制服
- possibly ひょっとすると
- choose ～を選ぶ
- tiring 骨の折れる
- time-consuming 時間のかかる
- express one's individuality through one's clothes 洋服をとおして個性を表現する
- relax リラックスする
- concentrate on ～ ～に集中する
- purchase ～を購入する
- reasonably priced 手ごろな価格
- provide ～をもたらす
- a sense of unity 一体感
- share ～を共有する
- various aspects of school life 学校生活の様々なこと
- design デザイン

> **Tips** よく使われる表現―確認⑤―

- Are you absolutely sure of that?
  （絶対にそれを確信しているの？）
- Have you got anything to back that up?
  （それを裏付けるものは何かあるの？）
- Are you certain about that?
  （それを確信しているの？）
- How can you be so sure of that?
  （どうやればそんなに確信が持てるの？）

◆ その他の表現

- I don't think so.
  （私はそうは思わない。）
- in addition
  （さらに）
- do you mean ～ ?
  （～ということなの？）
- plus
  （その上）
- perhaps you're right, but ～
  （たぶんそうかもしれないが～）
- besides
  （さらに）

ケース45　制服？　私服？

◆すぐに使える表現　Possible Opinions

☐ If students dress alike, they are perceived as alike. Therefore, it's easier to feel a sense of unity as a school.
（もし生徒が同じような服装をすれば、同じように見られる。そのため、学校としての一体感を味わいやすい。）

☐ Students learn to take responsibility for their appearance by wearing their own clothes.
（生徒は私服を着ることで外見に責任を持つようになる。）

☐ Schools should set a dress code.
（学校は服装規定を定めるべきである。）

☐ Students can express their feelings through the clothes that they wear.
（生徒は身につける服をとおして自己表現ができる。）

☐ Some students don't like to wear their school uniform just because of its unfashionable design.
（ファッション性のないデザインのせいで自分の学校の制服を着たがらない生徒がいる。）

ケース 46 都会生活？　田舎生活？
Track 46 City life or country life?

都会生活と田舎生活との間には、価値観や日常生活に違いがある。退職後どちらがより好まれるのだろうか。

ダイアローグ / Dialogue

TV anchor: "Where do you want to live when you **retire**, in the city or in the **countryside**?" In a survey regarding this question, married couples were asked for their **opinions**. Most men wanted to live in the countryside or resort areas. On the other hand, most women wanted to live in a **condominium** near an **urban** area.

都会と田舎、退職したらどちらに住みたいですか？この質問に関する調査で、夫婦を対象に意見が求められました。ほとんどの男性は田舎かリゾートエリアに住みたいと思っています。一方、ほとんどの女性は、都会近くのマンションに住みたいと思っています。

John: Which do you prefer, the city or the

都会と田舎のどっちに住

ケース46　都会生活？　田舎生活？

countryside? | みたい？

Diana: I agree with the women. Living in the countryside is very **inconvenient** for **elderly** people. | 私は女性に賛成だわ。田舎に住むのは年配者にとってはとても不便だわ。

John: Could you give me some examples? | 例を挙げてくれない。

Diana: Well, stores are too **far away** in the countryside, so you either have to walk for a long time or drive. Besides, trains and buses come only once an hour and you'll need a car anyway. It will become more dangerous to drive the older you get. | そうね、田舎では店がとても遠いわ。だから、長時間歩くか運転しなくちゃいけないわ。それに電車やバスは一時間に一度しか来ないから、いずれにしても車が必要ね。年をとればとるほど運転することは、危険になるわ。

John: I understand what you mean. But, you only **mentioned** the bad points of country life. In the city, on the other hand, you'll **miss out on** nature's beauty, the **peacefulness**, fresh air and **inexpensive**, fresh food that come with life in the country. Besides, I'm **looking forward to** grow**ing** vegetables and **taking nature walks**. | 君の言いたいことはわかるよ。でも、君は田舎の生活の悪い部分だけ言っているよ。一方都会では、田舎の生活につきものの自然の美しさ、落ち着き、新鮮な空気、安価で新鮮な食べ物を味わうチャンスを見逃しているよ。さらに、僕は野菜を作ることと自然の中を散歩することを楽しみにしているんだ。

Diana: You may say so, but it will get **physically** difficult to grow vegetables when you get older. Without a doubt, growing vegetables is hard work **no matter how** old you are. | そう言うかもしれないけど、年をとれば、野菜を作ることは肉体的にきつくなるわ。間違いなく、野菜作りは、何歳になっても、きつい仕事だから。

John: Physically difficult? Yes. But, by growing vegetables, for example, I can enjoy a **spiritual fulfillment** that one doesn't get from **material comforts**.

肉体的にきついだって？そうだね。でも、例えば、野菜を作ることによって、人が物の豊かさからでは得られない、心の豊かさが得られるのさ。

Diana: I can say for sure that it's possible to enjoy both **spiritual and materialistic fulfillment** living in the city. It's because we can enjoy spiritually relaxing events or classes like yoga, and we can enjoy materialistic pleasures such as musicals, movies and the like. I definitely prefer the city life.

都会では、心の豊かさとものの豊かさの両方の生活を楽しむことが可能だと断言できるわ。心からリラックスできる行事やヨガのようなクラスを楽しむことができるし、ミュージカル、映画などのような物の豊かさを楽しむこともできるからよ。私は絶対に、都会生活がいいわ。

Words & Phrases

- retire　退職する
- countryside　田舎
- opinion　意見
- condominium　分譲マンション
- urban　都市の
- inconvenient　不便な
- elderly　年配の
- far away　遠く離れた
- mention　〜に言及する
- miss out on 〜　〜を見逃す
- peacefulness　穏やかさ
- inexpensive　安価な
- look forward to 〜ing　〜を楽しみに待つ
- take nature walks　自然の中を散歩する
- physically　肉体的に
- no matter how 〜　どんなに〜であろうとも
- spiritual fulfillment　精神的充足
- material comfort　物質的な快適さ
- spiritual and materialistic fulfillment　精神的にも物質的にも満足感を得ること

ケース46　都会生活？　田舎生活？

Tips　よく使われる表現—強調④—

☐ I can say for sure that ~
（~であると断言できる）
☐ There's no doubt about it.
（それについては間違いない。）
☐ there's no question that ~
（~であることに疑いの余地はない）
☐ without a doubt
（間違いなく）

◆その他の表現

☐ in a survey regarding this question
（この質問に関する調査で）
☐ on the other hand
（一方）
☐ Which do you prefer, the city or the countryside?
（都市と田舎とどちらが好きなの？）
☐ I agree with the women.
（女性に賛成である。）
☐ Could you give me some examples?
（いくつか例を示してくださいますか。）
☐ I understand what you mean.
（あなたの言いたいことはわかるよ。）
☐ you may say so, but ~
（そう言うかもしれないが、~）
☐ for example
（例えば）
☐ It's because ~
（それは~だからである）

☐ I definitely prefer the city life.
（私は都市の生活の方が断然好きである。）

◆**すぐに使える表現**　Possible Opinions

☐ I love the food, the people and the culture of the countryside.
（田舎の食べ物、人々、文化が好きである。）
☐ I will get bored with the slow pace of country life.
（田舎生活のスローペースに飽きるだろう。）
☐ I enjoy shopping and other leisure activities.
（買い物や他のレジャー活動を楽しむ。）
☐ In the city, there are many bus and train services available.
（都市には、バスや電車がある。）
☐ In the countryside, I enjoy the fresh air and water.
（田舎では、新鮮な空気と水を楽しめる。）

ケース 47

Track 47

猫派？ 犬派？
Cats or dogs?

? 犬、猫はどちらもペットとして親しまれている。ペットはどちらがより好まれるのだろうか。

ダイアローグ
Dialogue

TV anchor: What is man's best friend? Many people **regard** their dogs **as** true family members. To **attract** dog owners' **attention**, department stores have special **sections** for dogs. These sections sell dog clothes, fashion **accessories**, toys and food.

人間の最良の友は何ですか。多くの人が犬を本当の家族としてみなしています。犬の所有者の関心を引くために、デパートは犬の特設コーナーを設けています。これらのコーナーでは、犬の服、アクセサリー、オモチャやドッグフードなどを売っています。

John: I like dogs better than cats. How about you?

僕は猫より犬が好きだな。君は？

Diana: I like cats; I think they are very **friendly**.

私は猫ね。猫はとても人なつっこいわ。私の猫は

235

Sometimes, my cats sleep in my bed, and especially in the winter, it's so nice to **cuddle up with** them.

時々、私のベッドで寝るの。特に冬は猫と寄り添って寝ると、とても心地よいの。

John: I disagree. Dogs **are** more **loyal to** their owners; they always **greet** you when you come home.

僕はそう思わないな。犬の方が飼い主に忠実で、家に帰ると、いつも迎えてくれるよ。

Diana: You are totally wrong. Dogs often **bark at** anyone who comes near the house, even friends. They can be a danger to **unexpected guests**...especially **mailmen**!

あなたは完全に間違っているわ。犬は家に近づく人には誰にでも、友達にさえ、しょっちゅうほえるわ。犬は不意のお客には危険だわ。特に郵便配達人にとっては。

John: You've got it wrong. Dogs are just **being faithful to** their owners. Generally speaking, dogs are **helpful** in many ways. They are used in **therapy**, **law enforcement** and helping **the blind**. Besides, **dogs are said to be man's best friend**.

それは間違いだよ。犬は飼い主に忠実なだけなんだよ。一般的に言って、犬は多くの点で役に立っているんだ。犬は心理療法、警察、盲人を助けるのに使われているんだ。それに、犬は人間の一番の友達だと言われているよ。

Diana: That's true.

そうね。

John: I think cats are too **independent** and **anti-social**. They come and go **on their own accord**, and do **whatever** they want, even if you say "no." Besides, they **make a mess** in the house. Sometimes, they eat left-over food in the kitchen **without permission**.

僕は、猫は独立心が強く、反社会的だと思うんだ。猫は勝手に来たり行ったりするよ。飼い主が「ダメ」と言っても、やりたいことは何でもするんだ。しかも、猫は家の中を散らかすよね。時々、猫は許可なく、台所の食べ残しを食べてしまうしね。

236

ケース47　猫派？　犬派？

Diana: I see your point. That has happened with my cats too.

言いたいことはわかるわ。私の猫にも同じことが起きるもの。

Words & Phrases

- regard ~ as ... 　~を…とみなす
- attract attention 　注意を引く
- section 　部分
- accessory 　アクセサリー
- friendly 　やさしい
- cuddle up with ~ 　~に寄り添って寝る
- be loyal to ~ 　~に忠実である
- greet 　~を出迎える
- bark at ~ 　~に吠える
- unexpected guests 　予期せぬ来客
- mailman 　郵便配達人
- be faithful to ~ 　~に忠実な
- helpful 　役に立つ
- therapy 　心理療法
- law enforcement 　警察
- the blind 　盲人
- Dogs are said to be man's best friend. 　犬は人間の一番の友達と言われる。
- independent 　自立した
- anti-social 　反社会的な
- on one's own accord 　独自に
- whatever 　~するのは何でも
- make a mess 　散らかす
- without permission 　許可なく

Tips よく使われる表現―反論⑦―

- [ ] You are totally wrong.
    （あなたは全面的に間違っている。）
- [ ] What you said is not true.
    （あなたが言ったことは真実でない。）
- [ ] You are wrong about that.
    （それに関して間違っている。）
- [ ] All that is wrong.
    （それはおかしい。）

◆その他の表現

- [ ] I like dogs better than cats.
    （猫より犬の方が好きである。）
- [ ] How about you?
    （あなたはどうなの？）
- [ ] I disagree.
    （反対である。）
- [ ] You've got it wrong.
    （それは勘違いである。）
- [ ] generally speaking
    （一般的に言って）
- [ ] I see your point.
    （言いたいことはわかる。）

ケース47　猫派？　犬派？

◆すぐに使える表現　Possible Opinions

☐ Dogs are more familiar with people and good tempered.
（犬は人慣れしていて、気立てがよい。）

☐ Dogs are very useful to people as seeing eye dogs but cats are not.
（犬は盲導犬として人間の役に立つが、猫はそうじゃない。）

☐ Cats don't take walks. Only dogs take walks. So it is bothersome to walk your dog every day.
（猫は散歩にでかけない。犬だけが散歩にでかける。だから、毎日犬を散歩させるのは、面倒くさい。）

☐ Dogs eat more food than cats, so dogs are costly.
（犬は猫より食べる量が多い。それで、犬は維持費がかかる。）

☐ Dogs are very popular to keep as pets. A survey said they comprise over 30 percent of total pets in Japan.
（犬はペットとして飼うのにとても人気がある。調査によると、犬は、日本のペット総数の30パーセント以上を占める。）

☐ Cats are more easygoing than dogs and they make me happy.
（猫は、犬よりのんきで、私を幸せな気分にしてくれる。）

ケース 48 高価格のブランド製品? 低価格のノーブランド製品?

Track 48　High-priced brand-name goods or low-priced generic goods?

品質が良いからブランドを選ぶ人、値段が安いからノーブランドを選ぶ人と様々である。今はどちらが好まれるのだろうか。

ダイアローグ
Dialogue

TV anchor: Some department stores are increasing **profits** in spite of the fact that they mainly sell **high-priced, brand-name goods**. At the same time, some **casual clothing chain stores** are doing well even after the **sales tax increase**. The key to their success is to **cater to consumers' needs** by selling **quality products** at low prices.

デパートは、主に価格の高い、ブランド製品を売っているという事実にもかかわらず、利益を上げています。同時に、消費税増税後に売り上げを伸ばしているカジュアル服のチェーン店があります。成功の秘訣は高品質の製品を低価格で売ることによって、消費者の要求に応じることです。

ケース48　高価格のブランド製品？　低価格のノーブランド製品？

John: What do you think about brand-name goods?

ブランド製品についてどう思う？

Diana: If I **can afford** them, I like to buy brand-name goods. They have a **unique design** and are well-made. Brand-name goods will certainly **last** longer than cheaper ones. **They are worth the money.**

もし私に余裕があれば、ブランド製品を買いたいわ。ユニークなデザインで作りが丁寧だわ。ブランド製品は確かに低価格製品よりは長持ちするの。値段の価値があるわ。

John: I don't think so. There are some **low-priced** but **high-quality goods** that are also well designed.

僕はそうは思わないね。低価格でも高品質で良いデザインの製品もある。

Diana: Yeah. But, take clothes, for example. If they are both high-quality and low-priced, everybody would want to buy them.

そうね。でも、洋服を例にとってみてよ。もし高品質で、低価格なら、みんなが買いたがるわ。

John: What's wrong with that?

それのどこが悪いのさ。

Diana: I mean, everybody would be wearing clothes of the same design. It'd be like a school uniform. I couldn't bear it. I want to wear something different from everyone else. Here's an example! I bought a $2,000 **purse** two months ago.

つまり、みんな同じデザインの服を着るということよ。それじゃ、学校の制服と同じよ。それは私には耐えられないわ。他の人と異なる服を着たいわ。これが一例よ。2カ月前、2000ドルの財布を買ったの。

John: Really? That's almost the same amount as your **monthly salary**. Don't you **regret** only having $10 left after buying a $2,000 purse?

本当かい。それは、君のひと月分の給料とほぼ同じ額だよ。2000ドルの財布を買った後に10ドルしか残っていないことを後悔していないかい。

Diana: No, I don't. I **am** quite **satisfied with** this purse because of its **originality** and its **stylish design**.

> いいえ。オリジナリティーあふれるスタイリッシュなデザインで、この財布にはかなり満足しているの。

Words & Phrases

- profit　利益
- high-priced, brand-name goods　高価なブランド商品
- casual clothing　カジュアルな服装
- chain store　チェーン店
- sales tax increase　消費税増税
- cater to consumers' needs　消費者の要求に応じる
- quality products　高級品
- can afford 〜　〜を買う余裕がある
- unique design　独特なデザイン
- last　長持ちする
- They are worth the money.　値段の価値がある。
- low-priced goods　低価格品
- high-quality goods　高級品
- purse　財布、ハンドバッグ
- monthly salary　月給
- regret　〜を後悔する
- be satisfied with 〜　〜に満足している
- originality　オリジナリティー
- stylish design　流行のデザイン

ケース48　高価格のブランド製品？　低価格のノーブランド製品？

Tips　よく使われる表現―例―

- [ ] take ~ for example
  （~を例にとると）
- [ ] for example
  （例えば）
- [ ] for instance
  （例えば）
- [ ] a typical example of ~ is
  （典型的な例の一つに~）

◆その他の表現

- [ ] in spite of the fact that ~
  （~という事実にもかかわらず）
- [ ] the key to success is ~
  （成功への秘訣は~である）
- [ ] what do you think about ~ ?
  （~についてどう思う？）
- [ ] I don't think so.
  （私はそう思わない。）
- [ ] What's wrong with that?
  （それのどこが悪いの？）
- [ ] Here's an example!
  （ここに例がある。）

◆ **すぐに使える表現**　Possible Opinions

☐ Brand-name goods are not necessarily quality products.
（ブランド製品は必ずしも高品質製品とは限らない。）

☐ I want to buy clothes that fit me best despite the cost.
（私は値段にかかわらず、自分に最も似合う服を買いたい。）

☐ As for clothes, I would like to buy special ones such as those made for wind-resistance and heat-retaining purposes.
（服については、耐風や保温性の目的で作られた特別な服を買いたい。）

☐ Particularly those who can't support themselves financially should not buy brand-name goods.
（特に金銭的に自立できない人はブランド品を買うべきでない。）

☐ It's not good to buy brand-name goods just to get others' attention.
（他人の注意を引くためだけにブランド品を買うのは良くない。）

ケース49　独身？　結婚？
Track 49
Single or married?

独身者の言い分、既婚者の言い分は双方にある。どちらがより好まれるのだろうか。

ダイアローグ / Dialogue

TV anchor: The number of unmarried people in Japan is on the rise. According to a survey, there are several reasons for this. One of these reasons is that many are not **financially independent** enough to support their own family.

> 日本で結婚しない人々の数が増えています。ある調査によると、これにはいくつかの理由があります。理由の1つには、多くの人々が家族を養うほど財政的に自立していないということです。

John: Do you want to **remain single** or **get married** in the future?

> 将来は、独身でいたいかい、それとも結婚したいかい？

Diana: **At the moment**, I'd like to remain single, because I'm able to spend my time and money only on myself. What about you?

今のところ、独身でいたいと思うわ。というのも自分だけに時間とお金を使うことができるからね。あなたはどうなの？

John: I'm single now because I haven't met a woman I want to marry. I'd like to find an **ideal partner** someday. If possible, I'd like to spend my time with someone I love.

結婚したい女性と出会っていないので、今は独身だけど。いつか理想のパートナーを見つけたいよ。もしできれば、愛する誰かと一緒に自分の時間を過ごしたいな。

Diana: Isn't it **annoying** to live with someone else? Besides, I wouldn't **feel free from** family **responsibilities** and **obligations** if I got married. I don't think I could **bear** it.

誰かと一緒に住むのは、面倒じゃないの？しかも、もし結婚すれば、家族の責任や義務から免れられないよ。私には耐えられそうもないわ。

John: Now you have a lot of friends and you can go anywhere with them. Twenty years from now, however, many of them will get married and you won't be able to find someone to spend time with. Don't you **feel anxious about** growing old alone?

今、君にはたくさんの友達がいて、彼らとどこにも行けるよね。でも、今から20年経てば、多くは結婚するだろうし、一緒に時間を過ごす人が見つからなくなるかもしれないよ。一人で年をとるって心配にならないかい？

Diana: No, I don't. I'm too busy with work to even find the time for dating.

いいえ。仕事で忙しくて、デートの時間も見つけられないの。

John: If I were with my family, enjoyable experiences would be twice as enjoyable, and **grief** and pain would be half as bad. It is natural that we get married and have families. Don't you think so?

もし僕が家族と一緒なら、楽しい経験は楽しさが2倍になるし、悲しみや痛みは半分になると思うんだ。結婚して、家族を持つことは自然なことだよ。そう思わないかい？

ケース49　独身？　結婚？

Diana: John, don't **force** your ideas **on** me. For those who love being alone, it's **far** better to be single.

ジョン、自分の考えを押しつけないで。一人でいたい人にとっては、一人でいる方がはるかに良いのよ。

Words & Phrases

- financially　金銭的に
- independent　独立した
- remain single　独身でいる
- get married　結婚する
- at the moment　現在のところ
- ideal partner　理想のパートナー
- annoying　面倒な
- feel free from ～　～を免れている
- responsibility　責任
- obligation　義務
- bear ～　～に耐える
- feel anxious about ～　～について心配である
- grief　悲しみ
- force ～ on …　～を…に強要する
- far　ずっと

Tips よく使われる表現—感想・判断③—

- [ ] it is natural that ～
    （～は当然である）
- [ ] it is not surprising that ～
    （～は驚くことではない）
- [ ] naturally
    （当然）
- [ ] it is imperative that ～
    （～は必須である）

◆ その他の表現

- [ ] according to a survey
    （ある調査によると）
- [ ] There are several reasons for this. One of these reasons is that ～
    （これにはいくつかの理由があります。1つ目は～である）
- [ ] What about you?
    （あなたはどうなの？）
- [ ] besides
    （さらに）
- [ ] Don't you think so?
    （そう思わない？）

ケース49　独身？　結婚？

◆すぐに使える表現　Possible Opinions

☐ I simply don't understand why people want to get married.
（なぜ人々が結婚したいのか、単純に理解できない。）

☐ It's none of your business whether I get married or not.
（私が結婚しようがしまいが、余計なお世話である。）

☐ I don't earn enough money to support a family.
（家族を養うだけの十分なお金を稼いでいない。）

☐ I want to make the most of being single.
（独身生活を満喫したい。）

ケース 50 カメ？ ウサギ？

Track 50 The Tortoise or the Hare?

コツコツ距離を進めるカメと短期間で距離を進め、後はゆっくり休むウサギの物語。ビジネス界ではどちらのタイプがより好まれるのだろうか。

ダイアローグ
Dialogue

TV anchor: Do you happen to know the famous story of a race between the Tortoise and the Hare? The hare ran faster in the beginning. **After a while**, the hare became **overconfident** and **took a nap**. The tortoise kept walking slowly but **steadily**. In the end, the tortoise won the race. Which type of businessman is **desired** by companies, the slow and steady type or those **capable in certain**

カメとウサギとの競争にまつわる有名な話を聞いたことがあるでしょうか。ウサギは初め速く走っていました。しばらくすると、ウサギはいい気になって、昼寝をしてしまいました。カメはゆっくりと着実に歩き続けました。最後にはカメが競争に勝ちました。どちらのタイプのビジネスマンが会社に望まれるでしょうか。ゆっくりと着実なタイプでしょうか、ある分野で才能のある人でしょうか。

areas?

Diana: Which do you support, the tortoise or the hare?

カメとウサギ、あなたはどちらを支持する？

John: It's a very tough question. Both seem to have their strong and weak points. First, the hare's speed made him overconfident.

難しい質問だね。両方とも長所と短所があるように思えるけど。まず、ウサギはスピードで自信過剰になったよね。

Diana: Yes. Also, the hare was **lacking dedication** and **seriousness** in spite of his superior ability.

そうね。でもウサギは自分の優れた能力にもかかわらず、熱心さと真面目さに欠けていたわ。

John: That's true, but it's a **requisite qualification**. Many businessmen have to **have superior ability** in certain areas. Unlike the hare, the tortoise's effort was slow and steady. His attitude toward the race **deserves praise**.

そうだね、でもそれは必要不可欠な資格だね。多くのビジネスマンはある分野で優れた能力がなければならない。ウサギとは違って、カメの努力はゆっくりと着実だったね。彼の競争に向けた態度は称賛に値するね。

Diana: I understand what you mean, but I can't agree with the tortoise's approach 100%. I think the tortoise should have woken up the hare. In that regard, he lacked **consideration** for the hare.

あなたの言いたいことはわかるわ。でもカメのやり方に100％賛成できないわ。カメはウサギを起こすべきだったのよ。その点で、カメはウサギに対する思いやりに欠けていたわ。

John: You're sharp at picking that up. It's not a good idea to **find faults with** others though. Everyone has strong and weak points.

それを思いついたのは、鋭いね。他人の悪口を言うのは良い考えではないけどね。誰にでも長所も短所もあるんだ。

Diana: You're right. Why don't we think like this?

そうよね。こう考えれば

251

When on land, the hare can run **with** the tortoise **on its back**. When in the sea, the tortoise can swim with the hare on its back.

いいわ。陸地では、ウサギはカメを背中に背負って走ることができる。海では、カメがウサギを背中に乗せて泳ぐことができる。

John: **Excellent!** That way, they can **compensate for** their weaknesses by **utilizing** each other's **strengths**. Together they can **accomplish their goals** quickly and steadily. It sounds like a **win-win situation**.

素晴らしいね。そうすれば、彼らはお互いの長所を活用することで短所を補うことができる。一緒に、素早く着実に目標を達成することができるね。双方にとって、メリットがある状況だね。

Words & Phrases

- After a while　しばらくして
- overconfident　自信過剰な
- take a nap　うたた寝する
- steadily　着実に
- desire　〜がほしいと強く思う
- capable　能力がある
- in certain areas　特定の分野で
- lack　〜を欠いている
- dedication　熱心さ、献身
- seriousness　真剣
- requisite qualification　必要不可欠な資格
- have superior ability　優れた能力がある
- deserve praise　称賛に値する
- consideration　思いやり
- find faults with 〜　〜のあら探しをする
- with 〜 on one's back　〜を背中にのせて
- excellent　素晴らしい
- compensate for 〜　〜を償う
- utilize　〜を活用する
- strength　長所、力
- accomplish one's goals　目的を果たす
- win-win situation　お互いにメリットのある状況

ケース50　カメ？　ウサギ？

Tips　よく使われる表現―比較・対照―

☐ unlike ~
　（～とは違って）
☐ on the other hand
　（一方）
☐ compared with ~
　（～と比べて）
☐ by comparison
　（比較して）
☐ by contrast
　（対照的に）

◆その他の表現

☐ Which do you support, the tortoise or the hare?
　（カメとウサギのどちらを支持するの？）
☐ It's a very tough question.
　（難しい質問である。）
☐ Both seem to have their strong and weak points.
　（両方に長所と短所があるようだ。）
☐ in spite of ~
　（～にもかかわらず）
☐ that's true, but ~
　（それは本当かもしれないが、～）
☐ I understand what you mean, but I can't agree with ~
　（あなたの言いたいことは理解するが、～には賛成できない）
☐ in that regard
　（その点で）
☐ Everyone has strong and weak points.
　（誰でも長所と短所がある。）

◆すぐに使える表現　Possible Opinions

- ☐ It's difficult to bring out others' real strengths.
   （他人の本当の力を引き出すことは難しい。）
- ☐ We need to learn to help each other.
   （お互いに助け合うことを学ぶ必要がある。）
- ☐ We need to think about how to increase work efficiency.
   （仕事の効率性を高める方法について話し合う必要がある。）
- ☐ Working together can produce a better outcome than when competing with each other.
   （一緒に仕事すれば、お互いに競争する時以上に良い結果を出すことができる。）
- ☐ Competition brings out the best in people.
   （競争が人々の最高の能力を引き出す。）

付属の MP3 CD-ROM について

※ご注意ください！
付属のディスクは MP3 データ CD-ROM です。一般的な音声・音楽 CD（CD-DA）ではないので、MP3 未対応の CD プレイヤー等では再生できません。パソコンまたは MP3 対応のプレイヤーにて再生してください。
※2015年4月現在の使用方法です。
※パソコン環境等によって異なることがあります。
※iPod 等の MP3 携帯プレイヤーへのファイル転送方法、パソコン、ソフトなどの操作方法については、メーカー等にお問い合わせいただくか、取扱説明書をご参照ください。

【再生方法】
① パソコンの CD/DVD ドライブにディスクを挿入してください。
② Windows Media Player・iTunes 等で再生できます。
＊複数のソフトの選択が表示される場合は、画面に再生ソフト一覧が表示されるので使用したいソフトの「再生します」を選択してください。
＊音声・音楽 CD を挿入したときのように、自動的にソフトが立ち上がらない場合があります。その際は手動で再生ソフトを立ち上げてください。

【iTunes に取り込む場合】
※MP3 CD-ROM は音声・音楽 CD（CD-DA）と違うため iTunes で通常音楽 CD 等を取り込む際の「インポート」では取り込むことができません。そのため、取り込むための設定が必要となります。お手数ですが下記手順にて設定をお願いします。
① パソコンにディスクを挿入してください。
② Windows Media Player 等が自動で立ち上がっている場合は終了させます。
③ iTunes を立ち上げます。
④ iTunes のウインドウ左上にある四角のボタンをクリックするとメニューバーが出ます。その下のほうにある「設定」を選択します。
⑤ 「一般環境設定」のウインドウが開いたら、上部に並ぶメニュー一番右の「詳細」をクリック、「詳細環境設定」のウインドウになります。
⑥ その中の「ライブラリへの追加時にファイルを [iTunes Media] フォルダーにコピーする」のところにあるボックスにチェックを入れて、さらに下の「OK」をクリックすると設定は完了です。これで、MP3 CD-ROM を取り込んだ時の保存場所が設定されます。（ここにチェックが入っていないと、正常に取り込むことができません）
⑦ 次に iTunes 左上、ツールバーの「ファイル」をクリックします。
⑧ その中の「ファイルをライブラリに追加」を選びます。
⑨ 別ウインドウで MP3 の音声ファイル一覧が表示されます。
　（音声ファイルが表示されない場合はディスクが入っているドライブ等の場所を選んで表示させてください）
⑩ MP3 ファイル全てを選択して「開く」をクリックすると保存が始まります。
　（ファイル数が多いため多少時間がかかると思います）

著者略歴

森　秀夫
もり　ひでお

1962年生まれ。上智大学大学院修士課程修了。著書に『英単語・熟語ダイアローグ1800』『英単語・熟語ダイアローグBasic1200』、『全国大学入試問題正解』（私立大学編及び国公立大学編）（以上旺文社）他。

MP3の内容

時間：1時間29分9秒
ナレーター　　Howard Colefield、Carolyn Miller、Rachel Walzer
50トピックのダイアローグが全て収録されています。

MP3 CD-ROM付き　50トピックでトレーニング　英語で意見を言ってみる

2015年 5月25日	初版発行
2015年12月 1日	第3刷発行
著者	森　秀夫（もり　ひでお）
カバーデザイン	竹内　雄二
本文イラスト	杉谷　ふさえ

© Hideo Mori 2015. Printed in Japan

発行者	内田　真介
発行・発売	ベレ出版 〒162-0832 東京都新宿区岩戸町12 レベッカビル TEL (03) 5225-4790 FAX (03) 5225-4795 ホームページ　http://www.beret.co.jp/ 振替 00180-7-104058
印刷	株式会社　文昇堂
製本	根本製本株式会社

落丁本・乱丁本は小社編集部あてにお送りください。送料小社負担にてお取り替えします。
本書の無断複写は著作権法上での例外を除き禁じられています。
購入者以外の第三者による本書のいかなる電子複製も一切認められておりません。

ISBN978-4-86064-435-2 C2082　　　　　　　編集担当　脇山和美